Thomas Frederick Page

The Golden Fleece

A Book of Jewish Cabalism

Thomas Frederick Page

The Golden Fleece
A Book of Jewish Cabalism

ISBN/EAN: 9783337045319

Printed in Europe, USA, Canada, Australia, Japan

Cover: Foto ©Lupo / pixelio.de

More available books at **www.hansebooks.com**

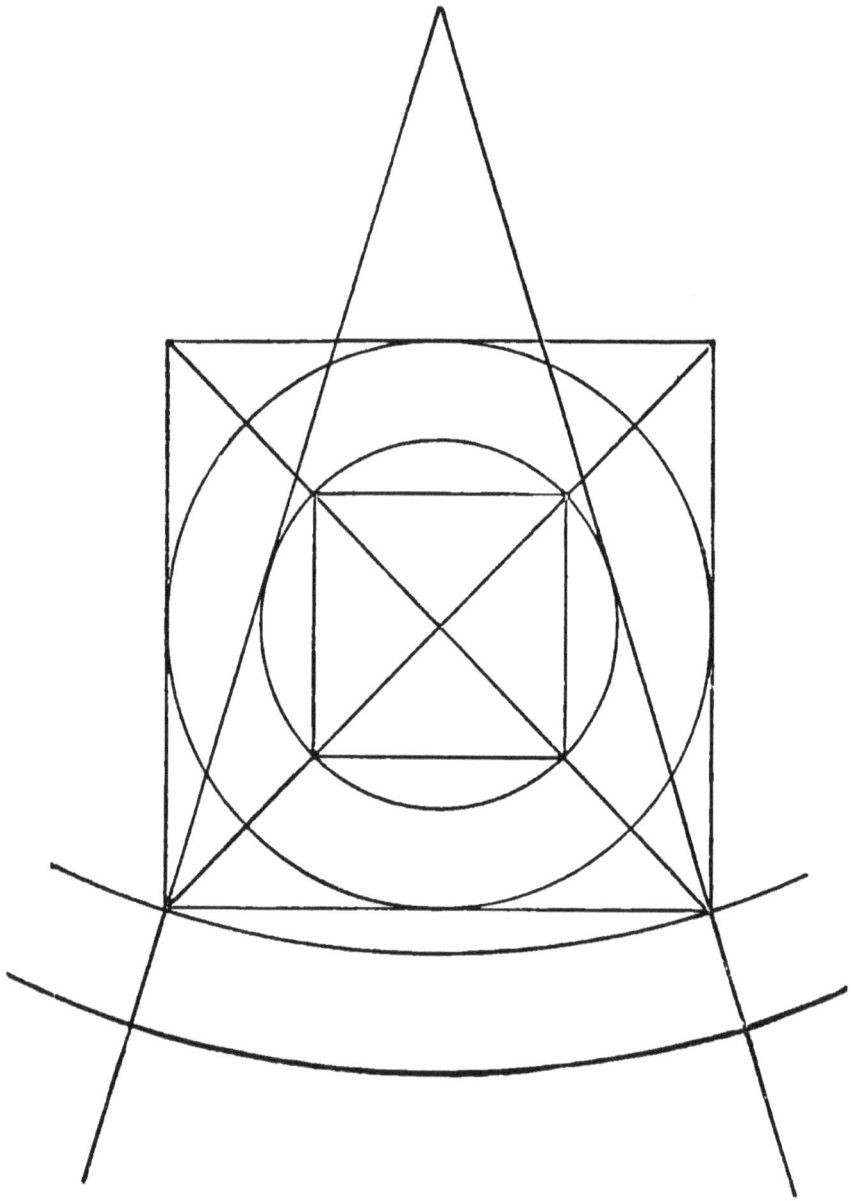

THE

GOLDEN FLEECE

A BOOK OF

JEWISH CABALISM

BY

THOMAS FREDERICK PAGE

———

LACONIA, NEW HAMPSHIRE, U.S.A.
PUBLISHED BY THE AUTHOR
1888

PRESS OF
ROCKWELL AND CHURCHILL,
BOSTON.

PREFACE.

FACE and reface ; the two ways of reading language from one print. The face of language, is as divided into syllables and words with one straight meaning, as man makes use of it in framing laws and transacting business.

Language has to have in it one exact meaning on its face, so man can read of what is taking place in the history of the earth and its inhabitants : any deviation from this, will result in never ending discord.

When language is analyzed, a deeper meaning is seen, which leads to a higher knowledge of the law of God, and of his dealing with man in that law. Beneath the face of language lays the Hebraic law, always and forever the same.

All names in pagan mythology are woven together in this work, and herein is found the method of reading the same according to the Jews of antiquity ; also the way of approaching the interpretation of sculpture as seen in ruins and remnants of past ages.

T. F. PAGE.

LACONIA, BELKNAP CO., NEW HAMPSHIRE, U.S.A.

GOLDEN FLEECE.

CHAPTER I.

HEBREW LANGUAGE.

HEBREW is to be extracted from any and all languages of the earth, and can never run out.

Every letter and utterance in language, has a meaning other than man considers as he makes use of the same in the transaction of business. They all have a high meaning in the great temple of nature, and there they are God's law as revealed to man.[1]

Letters are all syllables of themselves, and can be spelled by adding H, E, A, V, to each, and doubling V and putting Y with A and I.

U is a clean letter of itself, and its connection with all others is to spell it Y, O, U. As Y is the urn, and O the gateway to immortality, they are added to U, as the three are applied to man.

In searching for Hebrew in English, spell each word by letters, making them to express conversation as in *house*. Spell as H O you see. H is told to see O, and O to see H.[2] This is by accent. The reader is told the same things as the pronoun may be applied.

Spell *hours* as H oh you are S; S, becomes H in that way. This is but one way of dividing that word.

After spelling by letters, spell by letter and syllable in every conceivable possible displacement, and always accent the oh (O) and ah, (R) for there is the ohah (oar, ore) of the sculler, the

---

[1] The book which Hilakiah found.   [2] H is also told that it is C.

skuller of Golgotha. The difference between those scullers is
the sea, (C) and the K = the key; he saw the key.

To put a word into Hebrew, see what other word it contains,
and what is in the second word and so on.

Leave L, Leave N, leave H, leave I. Leave the second letter
of all that are doubled; double any letter that may be single,
add H, add one stick, subtract one stick, add and subtract the
crooks, add one I and so on.

Find the closest rhyme of a word, then the next and so on.

Find the dialect mix in a sentence, and discover how words
are joined together; *i.e.*, find a sentence which sounds most like
the one preceding it, as —

<blockquote>
Labor brings pleasure;
Labor rings play sure.
Lay brings plays, your
Laborings place, you
Labor in place.
</blockquote>

Thus one word or syllable joins on to another by a soft blend
until another sentence is formed quite different from the first.
This is the harmonious blending of all the dialects of the earth,
in which, lays the law Hebraic.

Man's life is set on the letter C, the cut circle. D comes next,
and is death; the next is E — the law.

Divide 120 by 6, gives periods of 20 years. Add 1 for the
sun at each interval; these are the tender points; the opening is
the Styx = Jordan.

a	birth.	
b	2 1 years.	
c	4 2	"
d	6 3	"
e	8 4	"
f	1 0 5	"
g	1 2 6	"

$$4,4\,1$$
$$4 + 5 = 9, \text{ the kat.}$$

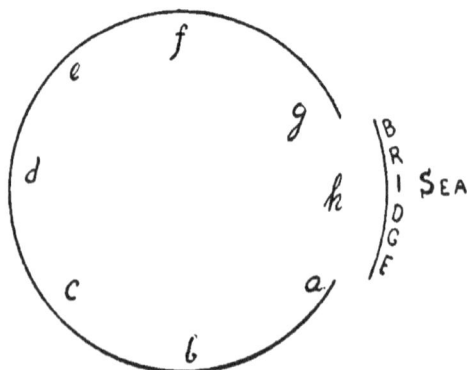

Fig. 1.

The bridge, is the reed, the way to read C^1 = sea, and where and when "read" becomes red. A is darkened as Æ — the difference between reed and read.

a	birth.
b	7 years.
c	1 4 "
d	2 1 "
e	2 8 "
f	3 5 "
g	4 2 "
h	4 9 "

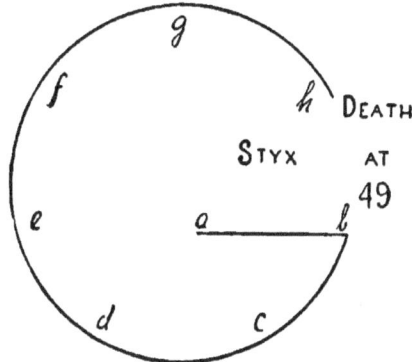

0 1|9 6

0 1 1 5

⊕ |1 5

⊕ 6

Fig. 2.

Add 1, 9 and 6, = 16 = P.

Add 1 and 6 = 7 = G —

— the 7th letter of the alphabet.

Add 9 and 6 = 15 = O.

Add 1 and 5 = 6 = F.

F is the 6th month Virgo, so

F becomes V sign Virgin.

This is the astrological birth and death unto a new life. The letter G (the holy biblical number) is the letter C with a bridge to close the circle from C to O; all together, spells C O G, see ogee ◡⌒ the serpent.

The point h, is where Belshazzar saw the writing on the wall, and where Peter went into the sea; see C.

This is the river Styx in which Achilles was dipped, and the red sea which Moses crossed. That sea is the fiery furnace, the den of lions, the hanging of Absalom, of Haman, the slaying of Joab, the trials of Job, the death of Saul, the suffering of Pro-

---

[1] Whether that life is short or long, the C is whole all the same, but by a closer division of time; as hours, days, weeks, months, years. In the example, the extreme limit is given so to include all divisions, and the largest circle of the same. A circle of 126 seconds is governed by the same law.

metheus, of Apollo, the fall of Adam, the voyage of Jason, and the place of a scull — skull.

He at the ☿ urn of the boat with the one ○ ℞ sculled across T = † that strait straight ; the difference, is the H G = temple and the holy seventh on which God rests the eighth.

The book of Esther is an ancient story of the astrological life, and death unto a new life, of Haman the A man. He lived his seven, and was the G man. As the octave dies at seven and is renewed at eight, he became the H man — the silent trip from G to A through the H.

He found Esther.[1] Est her, he st, by her rod, her — od — Herod.

He was Thomas surnamed Didymus the twin—Castor and Pollux. As the twin, he bear the names Mordecai[2] and Ahasuerus.[3] In this way, plow with the heifer and find the riddle of Samson. This is music of mysteries, and approaching the profound depths of cabalism, see a ☉, is M.

---

[1] Est ℞.   [2] Mort decay I.   [3] Hash of the whole 13.

CHAPTER II.

h A B e C c D e h E e F G e.
1   2   3   4   5   6   7

On those seven, rest the word Haytch; which is an add of the T and Y = the cross and cup. The E is with the A, only as Æ — meaning death. To continue the alphabet beyond the seven, as by octaves, the H is united with A, and the two as one, rest on the seventh. H A H rest on G in building octaves. This is the law as shown in Fig. 2, and it is the cause for a weak (wick) place every seven years in the life of mankind.[1] It is the step from G to A again.

One man chewed grass like oxen ; "seven times passed over him." Another labored seven years for Rachel ; in which word find arc and hell. A woman *bear* twins ; one was Jacob — see Joab — a Job, the other he saw Esau — U sea — C.

These are twins. Two lives of the body ; the life of the body with the soul, first, than the death of the body and the transforming of the soul into a spirit ; the second life of the body with the soul spirit replaced, and the additional spirit of the holy one also in the same body, is the mystical make up of the character of he who is the twin of many names, and the subject of mythical tales.

Upon these *seven*, is the rock placed which the builders reject. Here is the pith[2] of the subject, the foundation for Bible tales and they are all true.

When the Hebrew of the Bible is reached, then all is plain enough. The Hebrew is the easiest way to read those stories of Hebraic origin.

---

[1] 7 months, weeks, days, hours, seconds, the same.
[2] Pit H — Pi *th.*

A   H   O   U

B   I   P   V

C   J   Q   W

D   K   R   X

E   L   S   Y

F   M   T   Z

G   N

There is *no* Hebrew, but what more Hebrew can be taken from it. That language which is understood to be Hebrew at the present day, can be treated in the same manner, and it is all of it, the explanation of the explication of the connection betwixt this life and the life beyond the grave.

The history of the Jews is obscure,[1] for the very reason that

---

[1] Ob is S see you R͑ he — S cure, — the brazen serpent, the letter S on T, son †.

all races of men have in their turn been Jews and Hebrews,[1] as will be shown in this work. They are numerous as the sands of the sea (C), and scattered over the earth.

Letters were named abominations, at a time when people had an understanding of their astrological meaning. Abomination, is defined as odious. O die us. When a soul goes forth from the house of clay, it sees these letters in the light of that word in all of its meaning.

The present use of the word comes down from an age when the masses did arise against the abominable use to which they were put.

These things " which shall be an abomination unto you," are for Jews to study ; both the name and letter, and the thing of life, as the parts of that thing of life fit the law of language by names and anatomy. See the kidneys[2] are the kid (goat) and knees — the knee pans — the sign Capri. See capricious.

---

[1] Those who read double are Hebrews.
[2] Skimmer, strainer, sieve, riddle, puzzle.

CHAPTER III.

In the beginning was the word, and the word was with God, and the word was God.

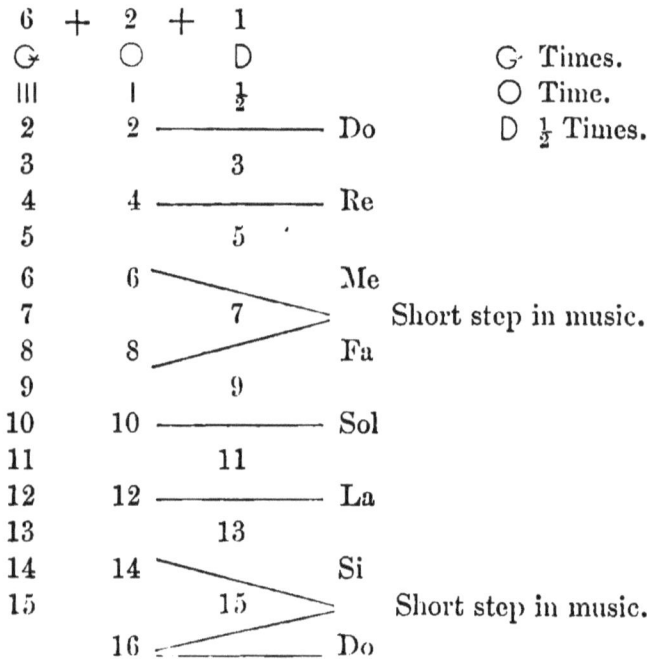

Even and od.	Even.	Od.		
6 +	2 +	1		
G	O	D		G Times.
III	I	½		O Time.
2	2 ————		Do	D ½ Times.
3		3		
4	4 ————		Re	
5		5		
6	6		Me	
7		7		Short step in music.
8	8		Fa	
9		9		
10	10 ————		Sol	
11		11		
12	12 ————		La	
13		13		
14	14		Si	
15		15		Short step in music.
	16		Do	

(Fig. 3.)

See Fig. 3. With G, there are three marks, because of the vibrating reed. With O, one mark because of the circle complete. With D, ½ is placed, because of the circle divided in two. Reduced to whole numbers they read 6, 2 and 1. Those figures added, make 9 — the cat. The cat, reads, see *sun* and *cross* = eye (I).

See why G is one, O is one, and D one, in the starting of the three columns of figures. It is easily seen how the minor scale is in this arrangement.

The III, I and $\frac{1}{3}$ are the foundation for the five senses of man. Call the fourth taste and the fifth ($\frac{1}{3}$) smelling. They connect the same as the O and D. The fifth, is the connection from bodily to spiritual existence. A person can smell that which he cannot see.

ASTRONOMICAL DIAL.

I.	A	March	1
II.	B	April	2
III.	C	May	3
IV.	D	June	4
V.	E	July	5
VI.	F	August	6
VII.	G	September	7
VIII.	H	October	8
IX.	I	November	9
X.	J	December	10
XI.	K	January	11
XII.	L	February	12

The difference between a square and its circle, is the amount of time that has to be disposed of in the heavenly bodies and their orbits, and is the law of destruction.

It is the foundation for the law of death also, and that fraction is the length of time of the death of the A man as he suffered in the silent H from G to A, after seven times had passed over him.[1] That fraction of time is the wafer and the seal. It is the eater piece in the H which makes the heater piece. There is the fruit of the tree of the knowledge of good and evil.

This same principle is in everything throughout (threw out) nature and must not be forgotten in reading this work with an understanding. Things are all ways changing from one condition to another, the same as the everlasting transposition of the scale by sharps. C G D A E B F♯. F becomes ♯. 4 marks = M.

---

[1] From the G man he became the H man, from the H man he became the A man, from the A man he became the B man = ⊕ man, see Fig. 7.

CHAPTER IV.

1		God.		
2		Unity.		
3		Trinity.		
4		Death.		
5		Lord.		
6		Virgin.		
7		Holy.		
8		Temple.		
9		Kat.		

$1 + 0$ Globe $\oplus$ $=$ O   I, A

$1 + 1$ Unity $= 2 = 11$ 2, B.

$1 + 2$ Death $=$ end .   3, C

$1 + 3$ Sun   M   4, D.

$1 + 4$ Son   N   5, E.

$1 + 5$ God   O   6, F.

$1 + 6$ Arc   P   7, G.

$1 + 7 = 8$, H

$1 + 8 = 9$, I

$1 + 9 = 10$, J

$2 + 0 = 11 + I = III = K. = \pm.$

1	A	Sun rise, to set.
2	B	Earth $\oplus$.
3	C	Cut life $=$ vision.
4	D	Bodily death.
5	E	Law.
6	F	Fan † P $=$ Pan.
7	G	Foundation.
8	H	Temple $=$ A opened.
9	I	Eye.
10	J	Janus.
11	K	Key.

12	L	Square = death.
13	M	Star of Bethel, the sun.
14	N	Son in heaven.
15	O	God, soul's passage out.
16	P	Arc, Ursa minor, pole.
17	Q	Second life.
18	R	Healer.
19	S	Serpent.
20	T	Square cross.
21	U	Holy ghost.
22	V	Virgin ✔ B ⦶.
23	W	Double LL, double VV, double UU.
24	X	Saltier cross.
25	Y	Urn, cup.
26	Z	Lightning, fire from heaven.[1]

Two P Ps are Ursa major and minor — the Dippers in the northern heavens.

All letters are absolute in the reading of the law of God, and always have been so from the foundation of the earth and heavens. They are abbreviations of heavenly language, and are all — each and every one of them representations of some part or parts of the temple of God — the firmament. The starting point is the bearing of the pole of the heavens; next, those signs which revolve around the pole, and from there to the zodiac, the great matrix of nature.

---

[1] From A to L is 12 inclusive. M becomes A, and X becomes L in a 24 months circle, *i.e.*, lap the alphabet in that manner by twelves. Y becomes A, and Z becomes ⦶. In the law of time divided by ten, K becomes A, and U becomes K; correspondingly, the letters set against each other in the blend of language.

CHAPTER V.

VOYAGE OF JASON.

Commencing on the 12th month — Pisces, the ash death and urn — Y.

		12	Y	Pisces,	February.
		1	†	Aries,	March.
		2	X	Taurus,	April.
		3	X	Gemini,	May.
		4	†	Cancer,	June.
		5	X	Leo,	July.
(Fig. 4.)		6	‖	Virgo,	August.
		7	†	Libra,	September.
		8	X	Scorpio,	October.
		9	X	Sagitti,	November.
		10	X	Capri,	December.
		11	V	Aquari,	January.
		12	Y	Pisces,	February.

Lapping Pisces gives double †, six sticks, making the weakest letter the strongest — the sign ⊠.

F sets against the month February.

The X crosses, in Fig. 4, are the experience of soul and body in being readjusted in the womb of the zodiac. They are the mountains in mythology. The square crosses are deaths.

In the wheel of fortune, the 6th month opposite, is across the *dell.* The strongest is Virgo, the weakest is Pisces. The same is heat and plenty, against cold and want.

In this circular dell, can be seen the foundation of many syllables and their fitting place in the temple of nature.[1]

As the cereals of Virgo, are the panacea for the days of want

---

[1] God's temple of time and its divisions.

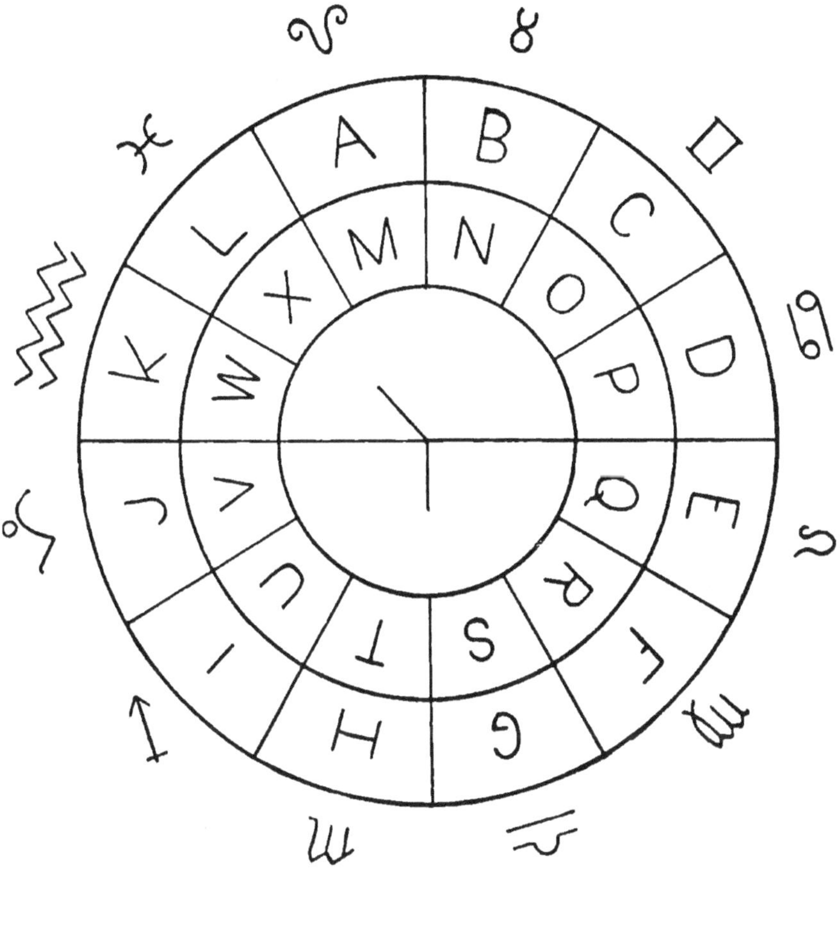
A B C D E F G H I J K L
M N O P Q R S T U V W X

in Pisces, so is Ceres [1] salvation for the suffering soul as it leaves
the body at the Tekel place between Pisces and Aries, the leap
into eternity.

Fig. 5 shows the current of life as it leaps from the feet to

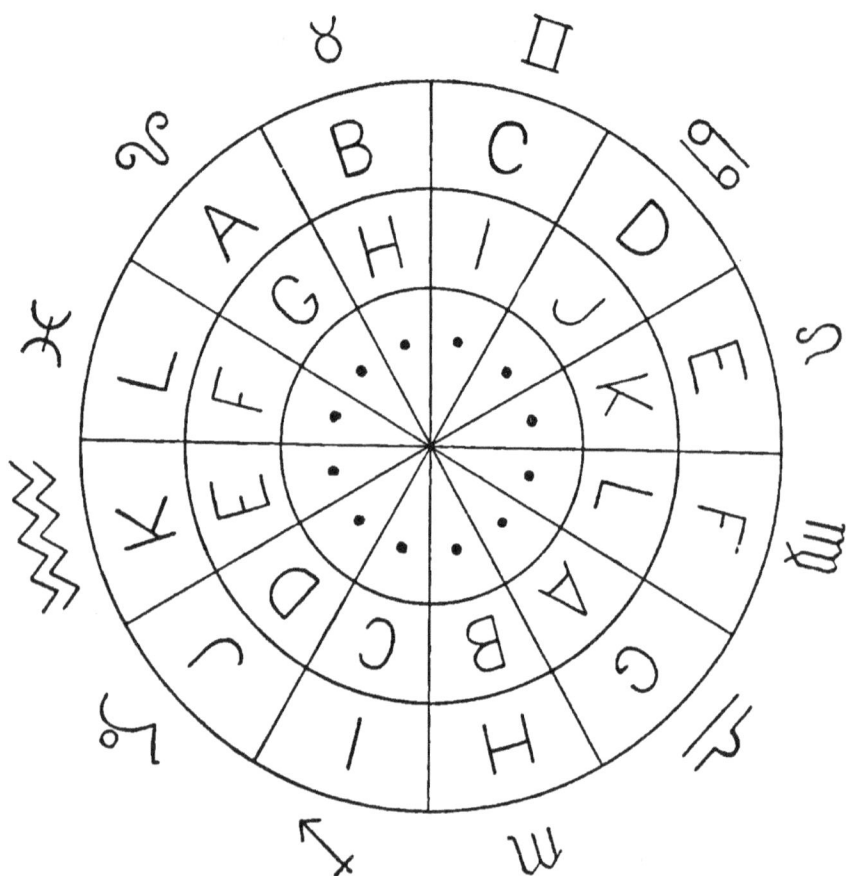

WHEEL OF FORTUNE.

the head by the moon's mean time, monthly. The roe [2] of the
zodiac is the matrix of the human race, and the circle which sus-
tains life, so long as the moon conveys that circle to the body.
When this fails to take place, the body dies.

---

[1] Ceres is the Virgin, the holy mother.
[2] The home of the syllables ro, roe, row.

To suffer this death and be put on to the sun's zodiacal course
of a year, is to be transfigured from off the moon's time, on to
the sun's mean time. This takes place periodically to a man who
is born for it, and he is the subject of mythology.   The sun

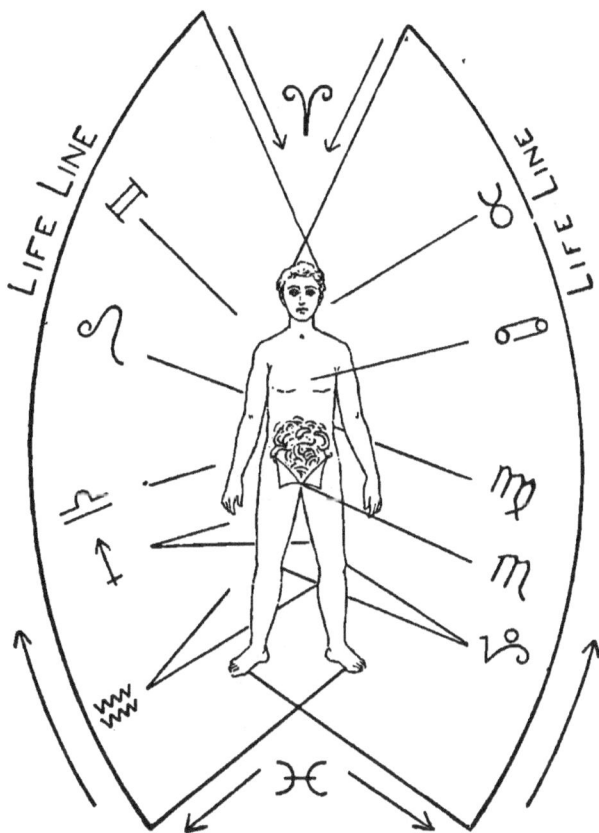

Fig. 5.

quickens the body into life again, and it starts on the voyage —
the cruise I fix on.

This is the great fish which swallowed Jonah = John A. From
this, is puke = ℞ you key he.

CHAPTER VI.

The letter A (A) is made with three sticks, and represents the sun and one half of the daily circle of light. The left foot is east, the peak is noon, the right foot is west. The stroke which connects the sides, is the line of light on the earth from rise to set. From set to rise is another A (A).

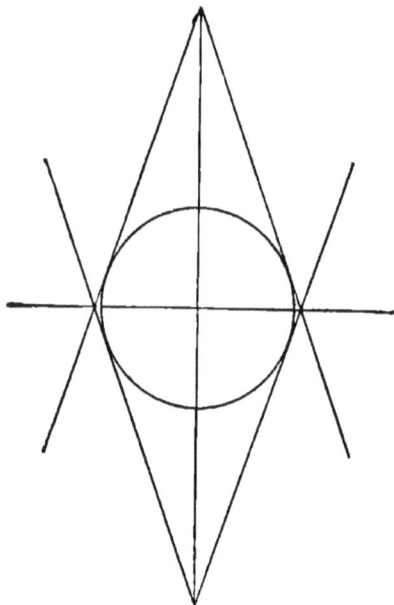

In Fig. 6, the circle enclosed within the double A represents the earth. The line through the center divides light from darkness, showing two D Ds; one of which is night for one half of the earth's time of turning on its axis. Thus A becomes D = ᗡ .

These two D Ds are one to the left = as ᗡ , the other to the right = as D ; the left one is east, the right one is west; the two together are ◐.

This law of division by D s, is because man's vision is limited to a D vision — a quarter of a globe.

Fig. 6.

Two more D s are formed by the sun's light as first on one side of the equator, then on the other side; these are the cross D D s. The four D s twice, make the bullock; see Fig. 7.

◐, is B, = two D Ds and the pole, ◐ separated, is IO. Two D Ds, are two doves. Two D Ds locked together as ◐, is a turtle dove. Two turtle doves, are a bullock.

Two D Ds taken from the top of two P P s, are pigeons; four of these make a bullock.

One ⊕, is a cherubim; two ⊕ ⊕ with the eye, is a seraphim = the bullock. To "kill" this bullock, reverse the word *kill*, as lik — lick — done with the tongue by way of explaining the law of God Hebraic.

The straight parts of the two P P s are storks — stalks — straw for bricks.

The storks lapped together, is the X; when opened, are (is) eleven[1] = ||. These two sticks are also L T V.

⊕ is B — the earth and poles. A, as the sun with ⊕, spells A b.

⊗, is the turtle, and shows six points of the compass; those points show the square and X crosses. The turtle is also the O X, with the pole — the pen of Mercury added, and gives A F H K N Y Z, — letters of three sticks. The belt line added, gives E M W, — letters of four sticks. The pen, is the fourth stick.

See D, is seed. The growth of this work is the fig tree. They who seed = see D, will reap of that which they sow — the shock of grain — the shock of the G reign.

C, see, sea, se, ce, ci, si. C represents the path of man's life from birth to death. Starting at a (as in Fig. 1), he reaches the end of life as at g, and goes to sea, see; goes into the silent H, the temple on high. The bridge is the line of salvation; the crossing of which, changes C to O = 15 : 1 + 5 = 6 the virgin, the holy mother.

The bridge laid across the cut circle of C, is the G round, and spells *ground;* this is ground for the body, and see (si) the sharp seven *th* for the soul, and is where it enters purgatory.

The course through purification closes up that line of salvation, makes the letter O, and carries to God; in cog, (see ogee) *re* cog nigh Z he died, recognized. In gear, the G hear, ear.

As ⊕ is a whole and reads life, so does D read death and shows one half. Add E, which does not change the sound. E is the Lord in the law, and gives salvation in D and destruction.[2]

The word devil, is D and evil; re verse *evil* and see Levi,

[1] A little singular about the plural read. Singular, is *strange,* when found to be plural.

[2] D becomes T in the cruise. D on † = dont.

whose house and home is the 12th segment — Pisces. At the end[1] of this month, Saul (as Levi) was struck by fire from heaven, and died the ash death; was put on the ♈ the urn and the *last* = salt.

Saul was sol the sun — son. He there went into the silent H as shown in Fig. 8. After the cruise through death and hell, he became Paul — ♇ all. Paw L the hand of Moses.

---

[1] End = den = Eden.

CHAPTER VII.

Ɛ HE. E, when written in *full*, is composed of four sticks of equal length, and will enclose a square plat when the cross piece is placed on the right hand side. It is the fifth, the law, the fifth house of the year — July.[1]

This month is the Lion; from which is Eli, Eloi, heloi, helois, helai, helais, Elias the lion of the tribe of Judah.

Elias, is the same as alias — he of many names. Square the Ɛ,[2] and place O inside, thus combining the words Lord God — ⊡. Add the fifth and fifteenth letters. $5 + 15 = 20$ the letter T the cross.

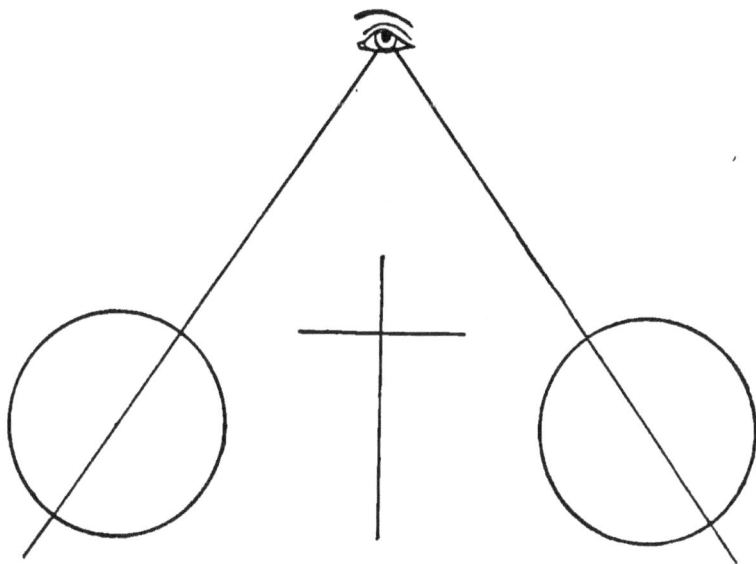

Fig. 7.

Remove the lower stick from Ɛ, and the left half of the middle stick, and F will appear, as it is usually written. The lower stick is the club, (jaw). F, is A, and △.

---

[1] Fifth beth. [2] Put the middle stick on the right.

F, when written in full, is of three sticks of equal length as f, and combined with E, is $\pm$, ef, fe. It is the sixth of the alphabet, of the week, of the year — the sign Virgo, and blends with V in the word *brief*, by way of $\mathsf{B} = \mathsf{\odot} = \checkmark$.

In the f of three sticks, bend up the end of the middle stick after drawing it to the right, then bend down the end of the upper stick, and P is formed.

F is the weakest letter, and is made by striking a diagonal line from the right down through the letter P as P.

This is the starting place of Jason as he went for the fleece; the first of the labors of Hercules, that light which struck Saul to the ground, the ash death from which rises the Phœnix, and the bolt of lightning from which springs the Sphinx; he who put riddles, but died in the solution of the one put to him. He thus solved it.

See Fig. 2. The letter G is the holy seventh. The part which is bent down from the cut, should be considered as swinging upward and past the end of the circle line, then back to the left past the same, then to the right again, and so vibrating in a constant hum, the fineness of which, man's thoughts cannot fathom. It is open at the left, then closed at the center, then open at the right — a circle then not a circle.

Here is the life of all nature; in it is the vibration of reeds, strings, air waves, and in any way by which music is produced, this law is realized as the sense of hearing.

To reed C, is to read O; to cut the O, is to smite the read with a reed. To reed O, is to read $\pm$,[1] reed D, re D as D. The reed between the 2 D Ds gives $\mathsf{\odot}$. The reed, is the pole and pen.

With G, place the chromatic numerals from 1 to 15 inclusive; all of the steps and half steps in music, and all the placements and displacements in and with the eternal rounds of life.

---

[1] $\pm$ ○ ℰ □ ◙ ◙. He who went through O, got the reed (read) and slew E the lion of July. In this way, read $\pm$ as the weasel of antiquity. The smite, was the time mite, as S is the serpent of time. $\mathsf{\odot}$, is the O and reed — the plumb read, plum breed.

CHAPTER VIII.

Fɪɢ. 8.   ⊢, is composed of 3 sticks of equal length.   It is the silent 8th letter, and the one which added to the seven, not only completes an octave, but it starts the next one by uniting *with* ∧ ; thus completing the circle of the gamut.[1]   In this way, ⊢ becomes ∧ ; shown by swinging the sticks together at the top — ∧.

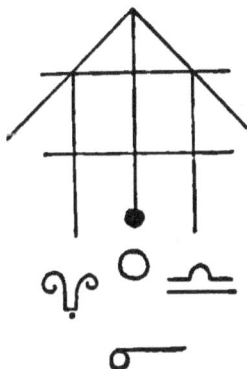

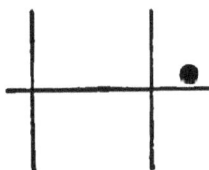

MARCH   SEP.
20   20

JUNE
24

Fig. 8.

This is the gallows upon which Haman was hung.   He died the ash death at 49 — the "seven which passed over him," and his soul went up into sheol, thence to hades and to hell.   He *re* turned to life as Ahasuerus and Mordecai — the twins Castor and Pollux.

Bend the ends of the right hand stick to the left, and B is

---

[1] Re ☿ head on the seven *th.*

formed. Bend them to the right, and the letter K is formed with three sticks, the third being broken. The difference between that broken stick, and the triangular piece with a dot in K, is the difference between G and A in the gamut through the silent H ; and the same is the cruise I fix on — the death of Haman and his transfiguration on the Mount at the heal of time.

H, belongs between all single letters of the alphabet, and the 25 letters all belong in H. The 3 sticks of Z is the 3 of H. The power of the whole, driven by God as *one*, makes the law of 4. He doubles as 8, and adds 7 to rest (re st) on, giving $15 = 0 + 1 = 0$.

See Fig. 8, *a*. By placing the A on top of H, the rafters and plate are added to the posts and beam. Here is Ah, the silent Ha. It is the Temple in the law. The vibrations of G go with it, and spell *gah*.[1] This is MARS HALL ; the great Temple of God seen and unseen in space.

In Fig. 8, the beam across the posts are the same in *c* as in *a*. Aries 20th, Cancer 24th, and Liber 20th. These are morning, noon and night also, on a closer scale. The death of the lamb in the sign Ram was the first of the 3 crosses. The death at the *king post* was the second of those three. The death on the right, was where the thief was forgiven in the sign Libra — the scales of justice. The same body suffered all three, the Phœnix came to life and explained the riddle.

The sign of the Crab laps with Cancer at the height of summer. See why crabbed is cross.

Face south to view those 3 crosses ; they read, light, heat, cold. These are the 3 of Golgotha, the place of a skull — the locality of the most acute suffering.[2]

In Fig. 8, *b* is older than the pyramids.[3] The small bit on the outer end of the beam at the west, hath the same meaning as that of the little bit on the upper right hand side of the lower case letter g.

The king post represents the plumb line — a stroke of gravitation ; that which struck Saul while "yet he breathed out

---

[1] P is *gah*. Pisgah.

[2] Suffer in G.

[3] Pyre amid, amid fire — the Phœnix.

threatenings,"[1] as by other names he died the death of the seven, slain by the hand of God — the bolt which makes a P into an F as P.[2]

Underneath the plumb is the well hole of death; from that well he came out alive again, and was a well man.

These three crosses are the three days (daze) of Jonah in the belly of the fish $=$ F is H. This is the well from which came fountains of living waters, and is where Moses struck the rock.

Each of these crosses are numbered 4. $3 \times 4 = 12$ L death.[3] The salvation of 12, is to add the 1 and 2 : $1 + 2 = 3 =$ Trinity. In deciphering the law which lays in unspoken language, the H is added or subtracted wherever its use or disuse will change a syllable in dialect.

H, is spelled as aitch haytch. It is the Aitch, A hitch, A H itch, the mange and distemper[4] of the ash death; caused by being thrown on to the letter A (the sun) and his course through the zodiacal womb of nature, instead of the same twelve signs by the four weeks' course of the moon.

This is the H hitch and itch (*it* see H) where Haman was hung with ten sons. (10 *suns*.)

The triumph in Taurus, and the case in Virgo, leaves ten of most acute suffering to add to himself, making eleven; the lap of Pisces made twelve, according to the division of time in that tale, and that which all souls pass through.

A gnome, is an inhabitant of hades. He is a G *nome*, waiting for a G *name*. The O is the hole of death he went through to know God; see that O in *gnome*. He is put on the A (the sun), and gets a name for the cruise I fix on; see that A in *name*. In this way, every word, syllable, and letter in language is placed in the law absolute for that journey.

---

[1] *th* re ate N in G.   [2] Bolt, is $\mathbb{O}$ all $\dagger$, $\mathbb{O}$ o square T.
[3] The 12 months' cruise of Jason.   [4] See liquid.

CHAPTER IX.

I is the 9th letter — the 3 times 3. It is the all seeing eye of Almighty God. No place is so obscure as to be shut out from that sight.

On a lower scale, it is the sun. It is the bright light of the A, where all souls are purified and pass from elfs to cupids by the A Œ A V.

Fig. 9 J, is the 10th letter, and represents the outstretched arm of the Almighty. See 10th, is ⊕ *th*.

J is made by placing 2 sticks at an angle of 120,[1] with a stone at the joint, and another at the fist, as in Fig. 9.

J is the initial letter of the compound JEHOVAH-JIREH: meaning the time of an advent — the altar of the son Isaac and the Ram. Isaac[2] was slain in the month Arez; he took the name of the lamb, and as the power of Orion the regulator of the zodiac, he is said to slay the bull because he suffers the influence of that sign and lives through it.[3] He passes to the next sign, and so on through the twelve.

The lamb matures as the Ram. That Ram is Orion, the head and front of the zodiac. By precession, each sign occupies the place of every other sign in time. The changing of names will always occur to suit the sign aspect of the heavens.

By the "signs changing places," is meant the time of year that the sun will enter those signs successively through the whole circular course; they change places, *by time with the sun.*

The fall of Adam, the circumcision of Abraham, the tales of Moses, Aaron, Joseph, Saul, David, Job, Jeremiah, and all the

---

[1] The name is different at different epochs, because of the rearranging of the heavenly signs — the place where the character of a letter sign is established by the relative position of the zodiac.

[2] Death and a naught O si fire — cypher.

[3] The soul of Isaac in space, and his body on earth with a new spirit in the neck.

principal characters in biblical mythology, are different ways of describing some of the experience of Jason during his voyage to the east. The whole has never been told in one tale.

The name David is the root from which all grow, because of the letter D, and the divided life. D is the 4 *th; th*, means fire from heaven in a manner of which man knows nothing until his death.

In David, is div A — divided by the sun's course.[1]

The alphabet being composed of astronomical characters of absolute time meaning, it follows that the story of 4000 years ago would not be the same arrangement of letters as the story of 2000 years ago, because of the difference of the heavenly positions of those letter characters.

The same name would not fit, although the same thing took place again and again; and here and now, the same as ever, history is repeating itself by other names partially, but not a complete change.

As the sun[2] man's time was placed on a sign for a time, his name changed to that sign; when onto another sign, he was assigned another sign name, and so on: a name for each and every sign under which he suffered during the course of transfiguration.

He suffered the influence of all the letter angles with which the sun was brought into contact for twelve months, and a lap of one.

He lived after death, and triumphed at the *last*, by having the name of the sun — as *son*. The sun was the star of Bethlehem, and as that star passed through all, so did he by bearing that name.

During the next twelve[3] months following, he suffered the phases of the northern heavens. These are twelve signs and a lap of one which give thirteen, the same as the southern phase; the two are twenty-six — the Alpha to Omega.

---

[1] Davy Locker, L ocker, ochre, earth.

[2] The "sun man," was *this* man. *This*, is the cross and I H S; his superscription.

[3] In twelve, is † double you, and elve = veel = *bell* by the sign $\sqrt{}$ which connects V with B = ① ; so from this twelve = L death comes the bell which is the church in the law of language.

Z, is the power of the whole; put the three sticks on to the circle of the whole, and see ⊠ — the turtle, which, with the pen, is the full power in nature.[1]

The end of this 26 sign course places the time at Easter.[2]

By this it is seen that it would require the cube of the alphabet many times multiplied and displaced[3] to tell a small part of the story. Writers of those stories were born under different signs, and bore different names. As they sought to write a tale in which was to be found a part of that life, they wrote wide apart as their stories ran, but the same could be found in all of them, by knowing the foundation.

The man who suffered these the most terrible of all things, was persecuted. If he told what he was undergoing, they thought him weak and breaking down. He was subjected to indignities, and cast aside as a broken down and a ruined man. He had to bear it *all*, and the earth has the history.

People found that they had been worshiping their own imagination of an advent. While he knew who he was himself, he was not allowed to tell of it, for it reacted upon himself.

The people worshiped images in the workings of their own imaginations. They imagined an image of the man, and they imagined the images and scenery attending an advent; and wherein the facts did not agree with their imagination, they applied the panorama of their thoughts which were of the moon born, always one faced and one sided, and he of the sun had to be despised and considered a man of less than ordinary ability. Men of college education were called on to decide that he was not their equal. That trial came before pi was square ate — Pilate. P on ♱ *us*. The tie was on P as ₽. See Pontius.

---

[1] He bear the name son, as the head of all other names, and with all those names.

[2] It will be seen that Easter relates to the double spiritual birth, and not to the birth of the body at the first. There was the birth of the body, then three births from three deaths, and the birth of Castor in the neck, the birth of Pollux as he returns to the head, then the birth as a spiritual twin. In this law man is mystified in reading mythology.

[3] D is placed, when turned from ꓷ to D for the sun man, and from D to ꓷ for all others of the human race.

CHAPTER X.

Fig. 10; ⊀. K, is the 11th letter, built of three sticks, and is from the Styx. It is ka kay kee ke key in Hebrew. This K, with the eye and serpent (S) is the kis of Judas; by double time (life) he was kissed and thus betrayed = ☉ † ray he ◗.

It is changeable to R, by bending the upper right hand stick to the left, and into a six pointed star, by shoving the two right hand sticks diagonally across the upright.

K, blends with A, in the word seek; see K, seek A.[1] This is the gather from eleven (11) back to one, the same as one leads to two. The same is true of the twenty-five, and thus the alphabet is a circle, always crawling within itself—"the wheel within a wheel."

When shown in full as at Fig. 10, it gives the sad iron, goose, and flat iron, by the indivisible part in which the hole is punched to make it equal, even, and divisible without a fraction.

It is that same bight which has to be gathered up in the earth's orbit at the close of each 2000 years of time. That dot is the death of the sun man on the even of time, — the wafer hole where the seal was opened and the veil rent.

This is the key to the bottomless pit; the same to hell earth and heaven, the same is with the archangel Mercury. These things are all of them material and real, the same as life and motion in any other way.

---

[1] K becomes A in division by ten, as P is F.

CHAPTER XI.

L, is the 12th letter, meaning death; the same as Pisces the 12th, the foot and *last* of the year. It is two sticks placed at

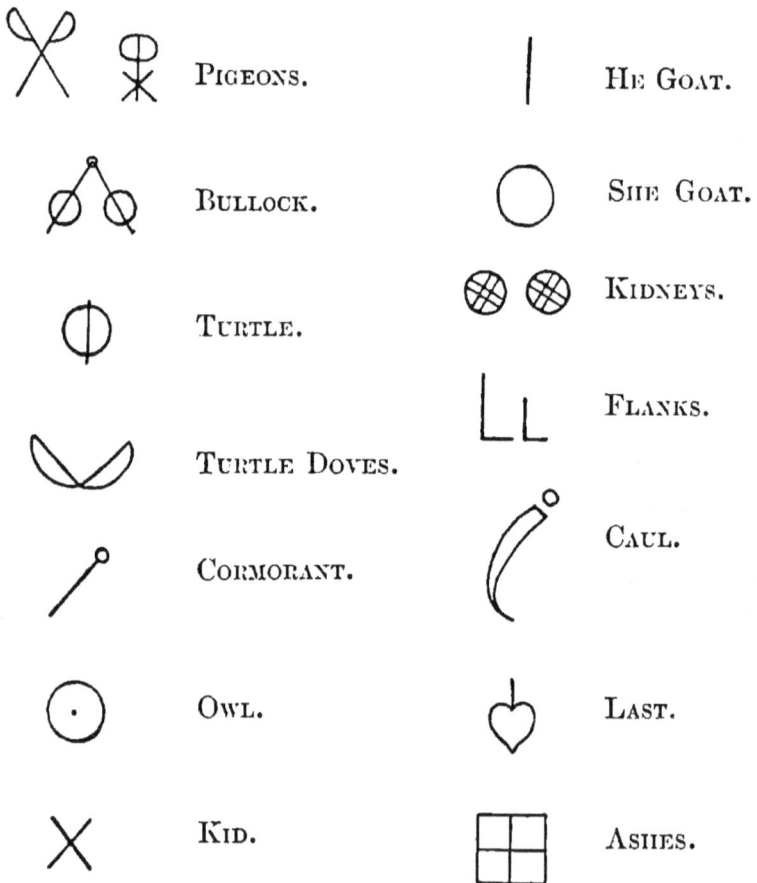

 PIGEONS.

 BULLOCK.

 TURTLE.

 TURTLE DOVES.

 CORMORANT.

 OWL.

 KID.

 HE GOAT.

 SHE GOAT.

 KIDNEYS.

 FLANKS.

 CAUL.

 LAST.

 ASHES.

Fig. 11.

a right angle, in which may be written eight (⌐8) ninety, (⌐90) or any number which may indicate division of time as differently measured in the several stories of the Bible.

It is spelled el, ell, hl, hel, hell. It is the *square* and surety, because of the certainty of death on *it*. It is one-half of the square cross, — two forming the whole. This is why two are used in *hell*. They are the flanks in Fig. 11, a destructive and a *cross* fire.

The L, is the lower part of the house where the cook, fire and *pantry* usually are, and withal is a broken spine and a square death. In *list*, L becomes T. List, is a lurch, and the edge in G, as listing, G I N = 14 listening.

The pantry takes its name from Pan and tri, and buttery, is from the four head of the Ram; for the obvious reason of the eat in G of the dip,[1] and the pass over the Styx.

Pan, is connected with *th* and ℞ in panther — the cat. The signs of the heavens are chained together with the links of the Lynx. The Lynx is the *keystone* that binds all together.[2]

The panther is a painter in backwoods dialect, which shows the eye instead of the H; H being allowed, gives pain *th* he ℞.

Pan re versed, is nap = the sleep of death; and shows that N becomes P.

M, is the 13th letter, built of four sticks and spelled em.[3] It is N with the reed added. It is the sun's (son's) number, the dose and doze of the baker's dozen.

The son's number in heaven, is 14 — the N. He comes to this earth as Mercury with the reed, which he puts on to N, and gives M.

The pin in the ℞ is the same, and wherever that mark is added or subtracted, or held in hand, and by whatever name it is known, it is the same magic wand which gives the double read, and the knife which mixed the colored coat of Joseph on the palate of his throat.[4]

---

[1] Eating of the dip, the sop = so ℞.

[2] All the signs of the heavens are in shape like some animal life. As they are all chained together, so all life is connected together by the law of resemblance; one example, is the thumb claw on a dog's hind foot being a connection with a bird's claw = see law = square *hor* all in. The dog has no use for that claw himself, it is the link that connects, and in this way find the links of the whole.

[3] Also am, hem, ham, hum, him.

[4] See ton sill, tom sill a bull — bell — bel — ble — ple — fle.

The death and resurrection of he of many colors, is why a colorer is named a dyer — die ℞.

N is the 14th letter, and signifies trinity. It is built of 3 sticks of equal length; these are the three sticks of A F H K Y Z.[1]

It is next to O in the alphabet, because it is the letter of the son when at home in heaven with the Father whose letter is O.

O is the perfect letter, and is the hole all must go through to hear the voice of God, and have an understanding of the whole. The word *whole*, carries to the letter O, as *hole*.

O is 15, N is 14; $15 + 14 = 29$.

In the key of A, O rests on N as the completion of a 2d octave, and becomes one for a start on the 3d octave, by uniting with H.

O is a circle of life. Two O O s are two lives. O (oh) is the same as au, and awe. O tom, the fall of the year, and the fall of man. In *winter*, find *re* twin win.

The letters T and H put together and sounded as *th*, have the absolute meaning of fire from heaven; which sentence means the power and acts of God in every conceivable way. The *th* with O, will be understood in the syllable *thom* as fire from heaven, (death to see God) and M the sun as 13. The A and S added for the 19th century, gives the name Thomas.

The fall of man, is all in nature with nature's God. The two O O s are not experienced without death to divide. There were two lives of the body. and in the second life, two spirits in that body; one in the head, and one in the neck at the core. These are the sacred twins of mythology. This is the transformation and transfiguration.

It is all done in and by the law of the astronomical alphabet, and that alphabet is in and of the great temple throughout nature. Those letters fit all of the known and unknown divisions of time, and all the signs of the heavens.

All divisions of time, are suns of time; the sea suns, see suns C suns. Thus according to the law of the see suns, sea suns, seasons, did the fall of man take place.

Adam was the A son, ⊕ son, see son, ☾ son, E son, the fifth

---

[1] Jews have the fourth stick in hand, and when added, is only *lent* by representation; the reed remains in hand the same. In *loaned*, is one all D, and the *tone* ad — one lad.

of the scale, sol — S all — Saul. The *re* verse of saul is *laus* = laws.

In *scale*, is time and lace.[1] In *lace*, is the square ace, the one spot — the sun, the star of Bethlehem = sol.

Adam fell and was lost. In *lost*, is sol and the cross — Lo s † . Just as plain as is the foregoing sentence, just so plain is the language of man set to that work. When he don't see it, it is the weakness of his ability to comprehend it.

---

[1] holy, hole Ƴ.

CHAPTER XII.

In the northern heavens are those signs which were the starting point for the law of language, and the means of man's redemption.

When Adam fell, God placed a spirit in his neck through his nostrils, and by this connection did talk to him, and gave him to know of a future life beyond this earth ; every 2000th year since that time, the same thing has taken place — the cruise of Jason.

Commencing at the polar star, the small dipper, little bear, and Ursa Minor are all one, and here lies the point at the tip of the tail of that bear — the *bar.*

This sign is a P, and is an F when shot through diagonally as P.

P, is the 16th letter, the number set with the arc of heaven. The two P P s, are the two bears, — Ursa Minor and Ursa Major, the Father and son — the visible representation of the unity as in the law to man.   They are to be read as Jupiter and Pan, major and minor in the principle of seven with one.   These bears are the bars.

In *minor*, see all that the word implies by the sound of it, no matter how spelled.   The same with all words which man can utter.

Minor, is the 6th of the scale as one, (La). It is the letter F, the number of Virgo, and the 6th of the week, (wick) fry day. See dirge music sol M. Dirge, is death I are G he.   The vibrating reed of G, is the mouth of the serpent — time.   In *serpent,* is time and repent. In *repent*, is ☉ ♇ he ℞ .[1]

At the point of the northerly pole of the heavens, is the starting place of the law as revealed[2] to man.   This has always been

---

[1] Ten = 10 = ☉ P he are — the little bear.

[2] Re veal he D — leave he D, calf of leg.

so, and has been given to people who had no knowledge of a future life by tradition. Whatever people or nation this man is born into, will thus receive the law from the fountain head, *i.e.* The visible heavens in connection with divisions of time, as shown by sticks, stones, and marking in sand.

Whatever name may have been applied to creed and religion, it was all the same. All suffer the influence of the signs in succession after leaving the moon's time. and is that which has been called purgatory.

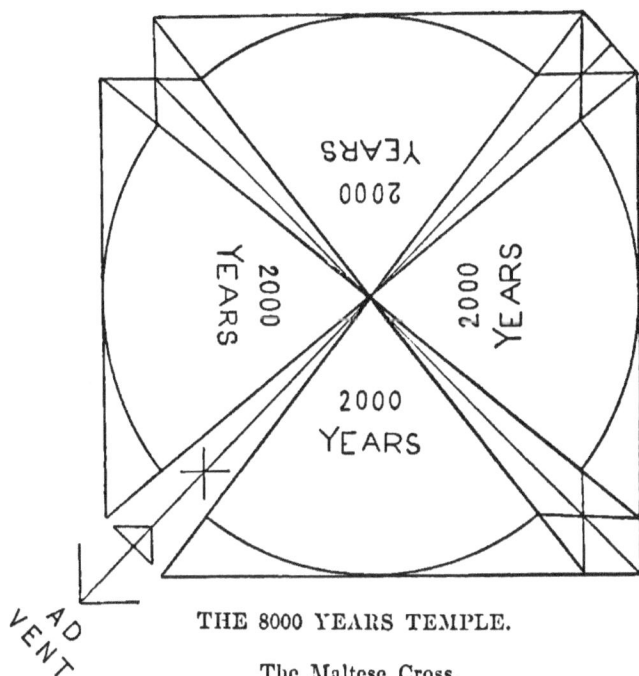

THE 8000 YEARS TEMPLE.

The Maltese Cross.

Throughout nature there is a connected resemblance, because of the chain which connects the signs of the heavens together. This is called type, and is the reason why letters are type. Type, is tie P — as ℞. T eye P. The same P and eye, is the way to rate pi, and is pirate. This word is with the word thief, as applied to two of the crosses of Golgotha.[1]

---

[1] G = 7 all go *th* ⩜ = sunlight as ♉.

Everything of life, whether cold or warm blooded, has its type in vegetation.

Type as applied to letters, has a very broad meaning. Twenty five letters with their combinations, represent all of the heavenly signs, and all life and motion throughout the firmament.

CHAPTER XIII.

THE shepherd's crook is a half circle.[1] In the build of language it is a bail. Place it on to the handle of the P and see B. Give ears to B and see bears. B is a representation of the yoke of Ulysses; meaning, July sees. The J being silent.

Two crooks make two B Bs of two P Ps. In one half of ⊕, see D, the cutting of that D in two, was slaying the dragon,[2] = beating the devil. Two of those quarters, give the son's crook; this is to be put on to a P, so the ⊕ is the cub; see you B. Tie the B Bs into ⊕ ⊕ and call them SHEOVAH and SHEVAH. Accent on last syllable. The first is she o bear,[3] the queen of Sheba. "From Dan to ⊕ a she bear" = Dan to B a she bar. The slaying of the dragon, and all stories and pictures of the kind, mean the cruise I fix on.

The statue of Mercury, is represented as holding 2 balls in the hand connected with a string, a magic wand, and a scroll containing the law. Sometimes with a stick surmounted by two wings, and entwined by two snakes;[4] or a stick with a ball on each end; all meaning his double nature — the twin, Castor[5] and Pollux.

Castor, is Mercury.[6] The man whom he goes into, is Pollux. Castor goes into the neck, locating in the Adam's apple core, brings the body to life and obtains control of the vocal organs. See the healing of the lunatic.[7] *Lunar*, being his time by the moon at the age of forty-nine, and *tic*, meaning time — as † I see.

---

[1] See ! ℞ see square he — ⊡.

[2] Two DDs are cut as ⊕ in slaying the dragon.

[3] O she bare. Vinegar cruise and side ℞ apple.

[4] Pallas, fallas, fall at the A and S; the Phallas, is two snakes with the wand.

[5] In Castor, see O and a star.

[6] In Mercury, see that M is ℞, and observe ℞ Y; quicksilver, the cat *th* heart tick. See in a bear = cinnabar.

[7] See Matt. xvii, vr. 15th.

The spirit Mercury returns to this earth once in every 2,000 years, slays the man who is already dying the death of the law of seven. He takes possession of the body, casting[1] the soul that was in that body into the great heavenly matrix by the path of the sun.

This is purging and refining in purgatory where the soul is sun fired, sanctified and purified; made pure by fire from heaven = *th*.

None can live such a life as to avoid it, nor should they wish to; for it is in the law, and is the way of progression from earth to heaven — from a soul to a spirit. Pollux suffered this, and all mankind must as they come after him.

The sculpture of old Egypt shows this same cruise. It is to be seen in curious head gear; a body of a man with a hawk's head, a man's head on the body of a bull or a lion, the griffin, the cone and circle, and all combinations of curves and angles on the head, and those things in the hand, all mean their knowledge of the periodical two spirits in a man's body, and that man's connection with cosmos; *i.e.*, the cruise through sheol hades and hell for the soul, and the deaths of the body unto life.

At the end of the eleventh month, the spirit of Pollux is back again in the head it left from, and located at the apex of the optic[2] nerves. It is a speck of microscopic size, enveloped in folds of gaseous matter in a cell of the brain formation.

This is one of the twins of May. The other (with the star) is in the core of the neck, where he utters language with perfect articulation, which the body feels the vibrations of as low as the sign Virgin. Thus is the body governed by the reins.[3] God rules and reigns forever.

The apple is the sun fruit, as compared with the moon fruit — the orange; the pear[4] (pair) unites the two. The going to the sun's time from the moon's time, gives the word apple, = the P P s and his ale, ail.

---

[1] He becomes Castor.

[2] Oh P † I see, optic.

[3] It is useless for man to think of comprehending any part of the incarnation. He can only think of his own body and its sensations as a comparison.

[4] Pear (with the crook) is bear; shot with the bolt, ($\wp$) is fear, fair, fare, F are.

A swelling of the neck is a goitre, from the words — goat here, goat hear, the goat ear. The goat is the 10th sign, shown as half goat and man : his ways none could account for.[1] His name was Pan, and he was this same sufferer, the moon and sun man.

Pan played the reeds in his first life, and after crossing the Styx, he played the reads, (re add S) the double pipe. He read everything two ways ; one for low, the other for high.

He also talked openly with man, and at the same time conversed [2] (in the neck) with the Holy Ghost, the voice of the Holy Mother : The body became the servant of the spirit.

Gap is pag, — the stretch of the neck. Pag and his N with the reed, is pag and his M ; pag and *h*is M without the D and H is paganism. See death and the temple.

History is his story. All language started from the voice of God as he gave the law to the first man : thus Adam gave astronomical names to all he saw, and made the application.[3]

David was this same man as can be seen by the names. He died as Uriah, as Absalom, as Joab, and became the wise man Solomon.

He bore the 3 days' pestilence, slew 3 giants, and took 3 darts — the D arts, and in many ways is it shown that he bore all of those things and became the double — the twins of May.

David took the name of Uriah, as Isaac took the name of the Ram. The body of David returning to life, it retained the same name that it was always known by. Uriah, is you are higher.[4] These things were well known in the days of those writings.

The great learning of those writers can only be understood by a long life of study by the principle of the gospel — the double read.

In the word *paint*, see pan, pain, and the cross.

In *pagoda*, see pag O, death and the sun — A.

---

[1] Ingenuity, in G, knew I †, in G he knew it = ⊤, in the seven *th* new eye †, Y.

[2] Conversely.

[3] Apple eye, see A tie on.

[4] Also the temple, Holy Ghost, and air.

One A, is seen to mean one half of a day circle of light, and
2 A As a whole circle of light — 6 sticks; so one A is the
same as D, two A As, the same as B = ⊕. This explains the
adding of A to D as AD — so much time. Add AD to AD by this
rule, and see ⊕ and W. The earth has doubled in the light of
the sun.

In *cherub*, find church, U R of the Chaldees, and hub; the
hub, is the north pole rout — the tour — T oh you R — the
T hour; the *last* suffer of that supper, will be understood in
the law of 12, when P becomes F by P.

Language is of God, and *is* God's. If he says *I*, it is *Ile*.
If he says *me*, it is *Him*. If he says *we*, it is the unity, and
trinity in unity. He, is Him, and Him is I. I is me and me
is I. I am God and there is no other. *You*, are mankind;
you is to be coupled with U as shown.

These personal pronouns are all allowable in the low language
of the earth, to express thought and do business with; they
finding their places as understood by one way on the face.

Great care should be used in reading Hebrew, by finding the
fitting place for all pronouns. Conversation between Father
and son, is the foundation of the whole of it.

CHAPTER XIV.

S<small>AN</small> † see laws, santa claus,[1] San T claws. Those who said "go up bald head," were the people of that race into which this man was born. It is a clause to show the pun *ish* meant of the Jews for persecuting him.

He was Elijah before he went into Pyrrhic fire. The *mantle*, is the article worn on the shoulders (the sign Gemini) and a shelf over earthly fire. He became Elisha, and the two were Castor and Pollux — the sacred twins. He was the same Apollo who drove the fiery chariot through the heavens.

From the hub of the arc is the axle, the spokes, the speaker who spake. The felloes on that wheel are the 12 segments of the zodiacal belt,[2] bound by the tire Orion, which is brazed at the "Tekel" place between Pisces and Aries — Arez. Felloe, is from fell O. From this is *fellow*.

Fellows standing in a circle formed the rim. They who stepped toward the center to speak, were the spokes men. The fire in the center, was the hub. In the "hub," was the *nut*. The nut, was ||| you T.

When two circles were formed, the inner one was composed of twelve and was the hub. The fire in the center was then the nut, the seed, the germ of life. This was neither wheel, nor fire worship; it was the worship of that great power to which people have always looked, for salvation in death. Those fellows had the traditional story of Hiram of Tyre, he who understood the wheel of time and the divisions.

He is the Master to-day, the same as ever, and the stone which the builders reject. He is also named Peter, and is the rock upon which the church is founded, and the gates of hell shall never prevail against it.[3] Tyre, is tire; meaning downward — plumb.

---

[1] Chimney is see him knee (Pan) the cup, see him nigh, see him bly, ply, fly.
[2] Bell † .
[3] See blowing up of hell gate in East river.

Blessed, B less ed, ⊕ less the E (weasel) and D : (death) a time after the wafer of the weasel, and of course after death. The wafer, is the fruit of the tree. Less the E, means having passed through the trial of E. Less, is square he S S ; double S is double time, two lives ; one of which is of course after the death of the body. Double time, is $\frac{2}{4}$. $2 \times 4 = 8$ the temple. Blessed, is also ⊕ less hed, ⊕ less the head it (the soul) was in.

The visions of Pan, is the Pan O Ram A. The appearance of the signs in the heavens which he sees on his way to earth as Mercury gives the word, and they are described in the book of Revelations, — the book of Asher.[1] Bound in heaven bound in earth, loosed in heaven loosed in earth : meaning that the panorama of heavenly signs, governs the history of the earth, its productions, and the fate and fortunes of the race.

P, is a B without the crook : struck by fire P becomes F the weak *est* letter. Week, wick he died, wicked, wick head, fire went out at Arez. See from death to life, the rekindling of that fire from the ignus fatus, that ignominious fate — F ate = eight = H.

Y P P F F E E □ ◙ ◙ ⚖ ⊠ ⊙.

Put the middle stick of the E onto the right side and form a square plat; □. Put the O inside of it and Œ is formed meaning death. The difference is as between a square and circle. The fraction is thrown out by punching a hole to even the two as ◙ ◙.

---

[1] A book giving a part of the life of he who died the ash death, and suffered the urn (Y) the two ways of the gibbet = G bit.

CHAPTER XV.

Q FOLLOWS P, because P shot into F, closed the circle of his life as O; the tail of Q, is his start from that O onto his second circle of life. He went into the great suspension in H air and was there hung. He saw things before and behind; so the back hair is called the cue = see you ⴹ.

It matters not whether H is sounded with air, for in it is the fine hairy gaseous threads of the Holy Ghost, the invisible power of God.

R, represents the serpent and death — a broken spine. The pin in the tail, is the pen — the club of Hercules.[1] That club with the upright is the two sticks of T.[2]

The ℞, is the same as ℘ when read as a monogram.[3] It is the title of him who with three names, went into that furnace which was heat one seven times more than it was wont[4] to be heated. One seven multiplied by itself — from moon life to sun life at the age of forty-nine. From those three names came the fourth — 4 *th.*

R, is spelled as are, ha, ah, iar, ari, air; meaning, are, be, was, am, is, ℛ; the latter, meaning the sun as the healer. Pull the pin and swing the tail to the left, forming B. Take away the crook[5] — the lower half circle, and P is left. P becomes F by fire from heaven as ℘. Tip the F over and remove the short piece[6] (enter) and see L T V X.

The letter S, is the same as a circle, because it is two half circles put together. They are twisted in opposite directions, forming the O G = ogee;[7] so S, is the sign of the serpent, meaning time and the track on which the house of God moves.

The reason of this is, that the firmament moves as one body

---

[1] Her cue (Q) square he time.
[2] The tail and pin are the X on ℘.
[3] M on o G ram.
[4] W on T is double you on †.
[5] See great owl.
[6] See little owl.
[7] Ogee is the form of the serpent.

on a path the course of which is the shape of the letter S. Passing along the same curve, joins the two ends on the line across its own orbit; thus S becomes 8 — eight = H.

This is why the crossing of orbits is X, and why H is the temple and silent here on earth.

Temples for worship have been constructed on the principle of divisions of time by this law. The Bible contains all of this method in stories.[1] The narrative, tale, story, is the high story at the tip of the tail of the Little Bear — the pole of the heavens. There is where the arch (ark) rests — Mount Ararat. The word *ararat* [2] means the law.

In the center of the figure 8 is the apex — the crossing on the orbit of the whole house of God — the firmament. The amount of time in passing over this course once, is 4000 years; but as the course at the apex is divided into two tracks, the 8 has to be passed over twice to complete itself. See Fig. 12.

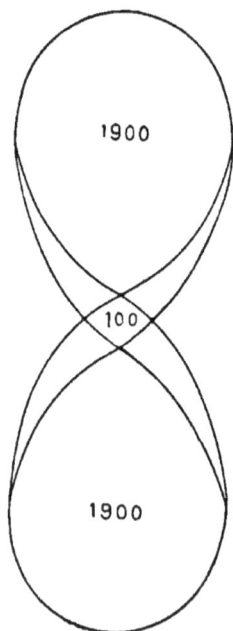

Fig. 12.

See 1900 years for one half of the 8 by single track, and 100 years of time in crossing the line of its orbit, making 2000 years. See the same for the other half of the 8, gives 4000 years all together. Passing over it again on the other track at the apex, gives a total of 8000 years: so 8000, is the temple of time.

The firmament is divided into two parts, and turns on its axis; that axis, is always on the track of the 8. The crossing at the apex on the 8, is at the division of 8000 by 4000, and 4000 by 2000. A crossing is made every 2000 years, and at these times Mercury comes to earth.

The law is always brought to earth at the time of the crossing at the apex — 14 years previous.

Twist the two half circles of B together and form S; use the stick of B for a bridge

---

[1] The hi story of history.

[2] Ararat is in narrative, and I V he added = I B he, as $\checkmark$ = B.

on the S, and thus form the Fig. 8; here B becomes H — the 8th = ☉.

The direction of the firmament across the apex of the double 8, is the same every other time; first one track, then the other. This "orbit crossing," is the time orbit; worlds without end.

These circles are all times, which are ended every 2000 years, 4000 years and 8000 years; whirled off and are whirls of time. Worl is to move by revolving, and D is the end; the two together, is the word *world*.

Language slowly undergoes a change, to correspond with the heavenly sheet of signs. Hebrew, is always and forever the same.

The earth has been whirled along on its path for a length of time which does not fit the ideas of most men at the present day. Everything is whirling along together on the great serpentine course of the twice doubled circle.

The time used in crossing the orbit, is 100 years; during that time, many things must happen, to compare with 4000 years ago, because the orbit is crossed in the same direction as at that epoch of time;[1] and some things will be the same as 8000 years ago, because of the same direction and track.

The whole firmament turns around like a wheel loosed on a shaft. The crossing of its orbit first to the left, then to the right, then to the left again, gives four lines at the crossings at the apex.

The word eight, is with the word height, eight, ate, hate. Adam ate of the tree in the height of sheol. He went up where all is fair = F air. His soul was an F up above all storms where he ate of that fare. The pure sun light burst his sac of gas, and he was cast down to earth.

He was cast into the bowels of the earth through a crater — an extinct volcano.[2] That fall, was a part of the same cruise from the influence of the earth and moon through the twelve signs of the zodiac, to the influence of the earth and sun through the same signs. This is Pandemonium; in which word find Pan, demon, the eye, the Holy Ghost, and M — 13.

---

[1] Same direction but on another track.

[2] Fall, F all, hall sun, ℙ aul son.

In *ate*, see tea and cat ;[1] in that word is the cross, the D [2] sun, the ⊢ and law. At this eating, the soul is taken off of the four weeks moon path,[3] and put on to the fifty-two weeks sun path, as shown in Fig. 4. There his sins all reappear to him again, shown on a panorama to himself and to purified spirits. His sins all register during his life, so he sees them all reproduced after he leaves the body. Everything is exposed and made known. There and then he eats of the tree of the knowledge of good and evil.

In the word knowledge, is know K now the square edge. The edge is the ax,[4] tomy ock, acts of God in the application of the law in justice — just ice the pole rout — ℞ out.

---

[1] Tea cannot be pronounced except as T, where the fruit was eaten — cat — N — he ten = 10 = ① Ursa Minor.

[2] D is A̶ as ⟁ a half circle of light.

[3] Crescent two quarters and full.

[4] Act, is cat, see † in the sun = A.

CHAPTER XVI.

The fall of the year and of man, is autumn — awe tom ; automatic,[1] is mathematics of the same. Souls cannot know the immensity of these mysteries until their finger of time points to the holes in the hands feet and side.

The feet locked and pierced, is the ash death at and between Pisces and Arez on the 30th, that day of which man has none but this explanation. The holes in the hands, is the doubled suffering in Gemini the twins. The spear in the side, is death in Cancer and the taking of the rib which Jews can now have to work in these cabalistic mysteries. The five holes are □ the weasel in the Jewish alphabet. Four corners and the center.

In the tale of THIS man as Thomas, he would not, because he could not believe, until he went through those things. When the word *believe*[2] is put on the altar, it will be seen that all man can have, is hope in faith, because of his organism.

God says you (U) to every animate and inanimate thing. He does[3] it with the D, and in that way you are *youd* — chewed — Jewed. See why J is silent. Beside the U, there is nothing for you in *you*, except[4] the Y O.

Est, is in East and West, the difference betwixt those words of the horizontal bar, is the W and A. A doubles by appearing again in the East. God says double you (W) to the sun, and the voice is double U. So W doubles, and is two double UUs ; the two with the pen make the yoke. When Y becomes J, yoke is joke. When see H (c h) is J, then comes the choke of being well hung in the H.

God says double you to W, and makes 4 V s — 4 × 5 = 20 = T. He doubles T in the same way, and the 4 V s become 8 V s, which are seen to be 4 double V s = 〰 the sign of Aquarius — Jove — Janus.

---

[1] O tom (attic) a tic of time, atom.
[2] See Bee and Levi.
[3] Dose.
[4] X see he P T — except.

Est, is he st, $=$ $♄$. Time and a crossing. Est is set. The sun is said to set. Set is see T. So the sun is forever esting, est in G $=$ he sting. Sting, is T sing. Sing, is S in G. Sin, is time in $=$ the serpent swallows. In the word cursed,

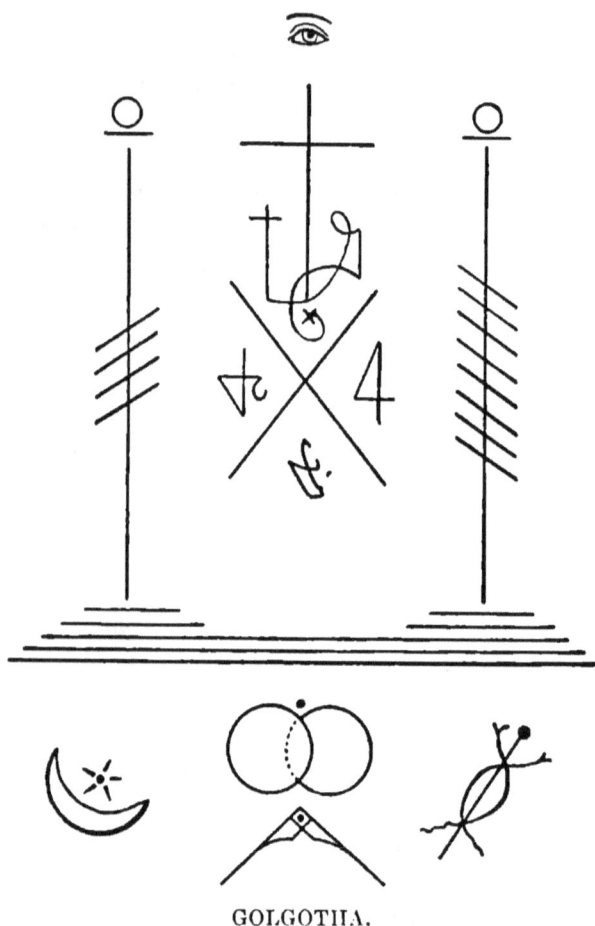

GOLGOTHA.

you are time he D — the end of time. Time is continually ending and asting; a light D and a dark $D = ◐$.

A glance at this earth from the hub, explains the lay of language, and how things are XD or crossed out by the procession of the equinoxes. X is a section of the Pan toe gra ph, and the shears — time hears and clips the sheep. Time H double he $♇$, spells sheep. So does all language carry beyond the grave, and the soul goes with the burden. The distance through to shame, is as a veil of tissue. One leap,[1] and all is clear.

"And there was war in heaven." Heaven reaches to earth. Mercury comes with the keys to heaven and hell; those keys are knowledge of the law, and the means by which he returns from hell to earth and from hence to high heaven.

He gives the law in a way suited to the race into which he comes; and whether in one race or in another, the same law is given in the language which that people use, and they become a peculiar people unto the Lord God. They become the Jews for the next 2000 years.

The word *Jew*, is of the jaw, chaw, chew, chews, chose, chosen, and is of the eating of the tree and its forbidden fruit at the close of every 2000 years of time. He who eats, becomes the first man and woe man — the womb man he V, — EVE.

The jawbone of Samson was the same.[2] Phili's tine, was the suffering in Saggiti — the bow man, the arc he ℞ = archer. One thousand, is on E thou son die.[3]

The bowman of no V ember shoots across the dell into any day or minute of the year. Phillip is the November apostle — the sun man in that month — Samson.   •

The body got no V ember; the soul got the ⊠ embers on which is the longitude and latitude of the mesh, the net on which all are gilled— gil D, guilt T, guilty.[4] See T and X crosses, Fig. 4.

The cheek of the jaw, is the chop; chops, is Cheops. It was the jaw of the *ass*, because of the sun and doubled time in that word. He rode through fire on those letters to G rue salem.

The rib of Adam was the system he was married to, and that with which he wrote the law. ℞ I ◑ is the rib; the pen is the style O. Style, is ⚕ lye the mash = M ash. See the signs

---

[1] Leap is apple, clear see L ear — real.

[2] Samson was the A and S man doubled.

[3] By Phili's tine he slew one thousand M he N by the law of leave N = 11. 1000 = one *th* O you sun = son die. Phillip, is the foundation for philology, as phil all ogee, he who died as od, hung with his nose against a column. ℘ ah I od, period, dot, ◖ ot, ▢. Philopena, is the double nut: the eating of which, brings the penalty — *pen* all tie, F ○ ℞ feet you are he = forfiture.

[4] G hilt hill ✝ ; the shiny way of gold, place gold upon the altar of words.

which are enclosed within the bones of the breast. In side, find
die and S, the time death.

The law was understood by the people of Egypt to the extent
of building pyramids; but they were believing in the records of
antiquity, and could not see the repeat of the history in which
they took so much interest.

Jonah was among them the same as Moses, before they had
any thought that they were in the D ark, and they knew him
not, and their ruin came. Ruin, is ℞ you in.

Lamb chop from the rib of Adam — his pen. The system he
wedded. His wife, Eve; darkness. Night to all but himself.

The Ram, was the name given to Isaac when slain on the altar.
He suffered the sign Arez the head, the place of a skull = Golgotha — G all go *th* A sun fire.

The male F actor on the left — east. His soul was out of the
head, and in hell.[1] This is when Castor entered the core of the
neck, bringing the body to life, and caused it to talk in an unknown tongue. Corpse, corps, (plural) core; the seed in the
core within the hull.

"Putting out the eyes of Samson," was the tearing out the soul
from the apex[2] of the optic nerves; the eyes were out of focus.
The spirit in the core ·prompting the body while the brain was
suffering a transformation, connecting the fore part with the base
and spine — the writhe of the serpent around the head.

This was the man at the stern of the boat with the ℙ addle
(paddle) — an expert[3] sculler, the skull ℞. The painter, was
the nose (knows) of the boat, the Atlas of mythology all the
same.

The double reed (read) of nature, is as light and dark, winter and summer; also the sun's path — 6 months one way, to
6 months the other way. There is no circumstance so small as

---

[1] See by the picture of the Hindoo deity kaal, that he (she) stands on her own
dead body which has the mark on the forehead where the soul was pulled out, and
the same mark on the live body to show where the soul was replaced. Four arms,
show the four ways of Janus and the cross. The masks, are the different characters she bore. Janus is of no sex known to man, so he and she will always fit.
See the word middlesex. See Chambers' Ency., vol. 9.

[2] A ℙ he X = 24 = ⅔double timer.

[3] X ℙ he are T — expert.

to be controlled by any power, but the power of God in four ways.

Man is so accustomed to nature, that he is looking for acts of God from some imaginary source, and does not accept a storm, or sunshine, as anything coming direct from the hand of God.

The names of all tools, as well as every other thing on earth, show the exact fitting to the work. Look at the "jamb" on a door-casing; it is a right angle, an L into which the square of the door fits, making two LLs; a place where flies get jambed; Jam bow *re*, the jam of Arez, Jambres — J ham ☉ Aries. The *re* bow jam of the zodiac and sun is meant. The doer cannot enter by the door, until he suffers the 3d letters in the words doer and door — namely the Ɛ; the Ꝺ comes first.

J becomes G in the word *jig*, and he says so. Thus G gets its soft sound from J. In *ginger*, see G in G, i.e. double G. Gog and Magog. M a Gog, S in agog, S is in *gog*, because S is an ogee, and so is gog G ogee. Synagogue. The land gage is colored to suit the painter.

He with the mix[1] of colors on his palette[2] is Joseph. He explains the double read to those Egyptians, the same as the two-pipe hautboy of Pan.

He bears all the names of the sons of Jacob, as Elias. He suffers the sun in Pisces, Arez, Taurus, and so on through the twelve, and gets sacked by those brethren[3] as he enters them.

He gets the Y in his sack, and is the Father of them all, (Jacob) as the sun is the Father of the yearly twelve months.

J a cob = Jacob, the cob that smokes ham. See O B the serpent, the cob S = cobs.

Triumphant in the month of May, he becomes the twins, and takes the cup as the emblem of death in the months to come.

The exact time of the 3 square crosses of Golgotha, will always depend on the position of the zodiacal belt with reference to the sun's time on the same, as crossing at the equinoxes.

---

[1] In the word *mix*, is the sun (13) and nine, — the cat — Lynx — that which links: also six sticks and the eye. Those sticks give the turtle, the ecliptic, the equatorial belt, and the reed in hand. This reed is a staff which goes with the sun, and gives the lines of Capricornus and Cancer.

[2] ℞ all ate.

[3] Breath ℞ he N = 14.

The interpretation of those three crosses, is the body of the man being adjusted to the line of the axis of the earth, across the line of the equator; subjected to the yearly course of the *sun* with the zodiac, instead of the *moon* with the zodiac as born under at the first.[1] The soul at the same time is cast into hell, and suffers the same cruise in space — the same adjustment, spiritually as bodily.

Man is adjusted to this earth, with his head and feet on a line with the pole, and his arms on a line with the equator. This takes place in pregnancy. He is changed to a right angle from that adjustment at the time of parturition, which places him on latitude facing west, with his arms stretched from north to south. If anything takes place in the signs of the heavens to affect his square cross, he is sick.

The soul turns summer set by its fall, and goes into pregnancy in a similar manner, bearing the angles of parturition as it bursts into a spiritual life. This is ☽ west and ☾ east.

The angle of the ecliptic with the equator, is the readjustment on the X, the saltier crosses.

Samson suffered all these things and got bar bard; his air was cut in space and the body came to life and health again. He suffered in the mounts of the soul's rising and being cast down again to hades.

He called the name of the place En-hakkore; the N core, the H a key core, the core in the neck in which was the spirit Mercury who came to the *foot* light again at the encore, to repeat the law.

Samson called fire from heaven the same as Elisha, and it is always done at the same encore. See story of fire-brands and foxes.[2]

Moses called fire from heaven, the same as Elisha. He was the *only* sorcerer in Egypt; others did pretend to know it. He stood under the inverted saucer, (sorcer) the dome over head, and gave vent to his feelings. See you P and saw saw he ℞ = cup and saucer. Saw saw, is the sign of Aquarius, ♒.

---

[1] All are born on the angle as square moon men, except he X see P T.

[2] By *fox*, understand F and Taurus. S cent.

Cain was the same man. He slew the bull. The ℞ in brother bothered him. Cain's cane, was the club of Hercules. He went to the L an D of N od — the od number of '3 sticks. Nod, is on D,[1] also don.

The nod is in the bow. He had to hold his peace, (piece). He could not speak it. He simply bowed to people as he passed them, only nodding, for fear of more persecution. He bowed to the inevitable.

Then God brought fire and disaster on to earth, so the people could see by names, figures, and dates, that what Cain said was true. This applies to all advents, and the history of Cain is always placed at those times, the same as all other names.

The knowledge of the double read, is art in brass [2] and iron.[3]

In Fig. 4, two parallel lines (2 sticks) are with August. This is because the Virgin bear up the sufferer through that month with ease.

Virgin, is the name for the female nature of God, and Jove for the male nature. Jove sets to the month January, and he is Janus — Aquarius the water-bearer.

Aquarius, is the fountain for the words water (aqua) and quarter, the 4 ways of Janus; the Q put with water is qwater, and is a "cue" to "cunning work in brass." *Light*, is quarter, and *dark*, is water; here is the divide in the law, because man sees but one at a time while in the body. When he goes to the "dark waters" he wants the cue (Q) to quarters. The cue will be found in the H, the air and hair. The 4 rivers of the garden, mean the 4 ways of the square cross, they quarter it, aqua it, acquire it, a quire *it*.[4] ℘ a ℘ he ℞ = paper.

Adam was in Eden where there were 4 ways to everything, but he knew it not, until driven out at the time of death. All mankind are in that gar den the same as ever.

The 3d cross agrees with the fall equinox : the male factor on the right ; these deaths on the left and right, (thieves) are represented as a man tied on at the elbows, because they were

---

[1] Became no D — triumph over death.
[2] A type of brass is tin and copper.
[3] Gen. iv. ch., 22 vr., was so called at that time.
[4] A cue higher it, ire it.

not so painful as the middle cross. The one at the right was not as painful or of so long duration as that on the left — the sign of the Ram — the head.

Look at the three crosses of Golgotha with the back to the north, and the first cross will be east. By coming to life and strength again, he is said to slay the bull in April. Here he was St. Mithras.[1] The meaning is again the same; he suffered the influence of that segmentary arc of the zodiacal matrix, and lived through it by suffering on the saltier cross as St. Andrew.

ADAM'S FIRST ALPHABETICAL TEMPLE.

Si.	Ta.	Ubi.
Tuh.	Spal.	An.
Sa.	Col.	I.
Fin.	Lugh.	Yew.
Too.	Fa.	We.
Twal.	Ho.	Nau.
Laf.	La.	

---

[1] Myth ℞ A and S of time.

CHAPTER XVII.

APRIL is one of the X crosses. These are the sufferings between the T T T s, the V and Y s.

The reason for the bar being let down on the T to form the cross, is because of the revolution of the zodiac. Those deaths will not always occur precisely on the same dates, but will always agree with the seasons. Otherwise the letter T would always be correct for the representation.

For this same reason will the names vary from one generation of time to another. People who are looking backward, are blind to the truth of history repeating itself. They are looking for the fulfilment of prophecies which are already fulfilled. Use straw for making bricks, and see 64 inches in a brick. $6 + 4 = 10 = \odot = $ B ah I see $\ltimes$, the key.

With these T s and X s, the soul mounts up to the upper strata of that which surrounds the earth ; this is the being "caught up into the third (*th* heard) heaven" where there are [1] unspeakable words to be heard.

The soul leaving the body and returning again, are mounts ; mounting up to be cast down again. The Mount of O live ; (olives) live R — liver. See Prometheus chained to Mount Caucasus ; his liver chewed by the vulture of time for 7 times 7 years $= 49, 4 + 9 = 13$ the unlucky number of the sun. His luck turned again and again.

The result of this one year's trials to the body, sums up 13 suspensions of animation, 3 of which were deaths.

Those deaths were not the cold dead and forever lifeless body of a putrescent substance ; they are unexplainable to man.

At the end of two years and one month, he turns in the matrix again so to fit the entrance to a spiritual birth in a northerly direction, and is adjusted to the polar line as its connections with the circumpolar heavens — the bears around the polar star.

---

[1] *th* hair R .

His head is now in Aquari, his neck in Pisces, and his feet in Capri. His arms being in Aries, is why he is pictured with a lamb in his arms. His crook is the half circle of B — P, and the staff is the pen. With the st A f f (staff) he doubles the F.

He is now in the matrix so that the weak place (life line) is at new years.

All mankind are on the 4 weeks' course of the moon, and preserved or destroyed the same way.

Once in every 4 weeks, aproximately, this same click goes from the toes to the head, so quick that the word *quick*[1] fits under the nails.[2] This is the circle of life by the moon's time, as it puts the influence of the zodiacal matrix on to the earth.

This circle of life is always closed or opened where the sign of Pisces joins on to Aries.[3] Thus *arise* from the foot to the head. The *last* becomes first, and the first *last.*

The difference between first and last, is the *fir* and *la*, which spell *flail.* The difference between F and L, is the small piece of stick at the middle of the F. That piece is the od day of leap year.

$$\frac{14 \mid 40}{5 \quad 40} = 9 \text{ and } 0 - \boxed{90} .$$

Adam's number on high being 14, and death at four and the grave being 40, is why mankind are limited to 1440 moons; which, with 6 sun periods, is the 126 years of life. In this period of time is a fraction to carry along; not a fraction of *time,* but a fraction in the law of division.

---

[1] Cue U I see key; the I here meant, is all those who read and understand.

[2] Nail, is the N ail: that sickness which carries as far as 14 = N by stopping on 13 = M = ※ = the sun.

[3] This preserving circle is the toe add, (toad). This is true in all animal and vegetable life. The to ad, two D D s ad, two add to T V. Add to E = D the dot = death ○ † and see the weasel hole all souls go through to salvation. The same is the ferret hole for one only; he who experienced the same thing in body, soul, and spirit — spirits.

Multiply the temple by itself, $8 \times 8 = 64$
Multiply the sun by the law, $\underline{5 \times 13 = 65}$
$$129$$

Fig. 13.

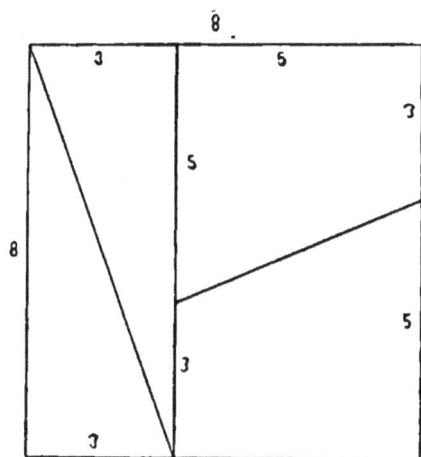

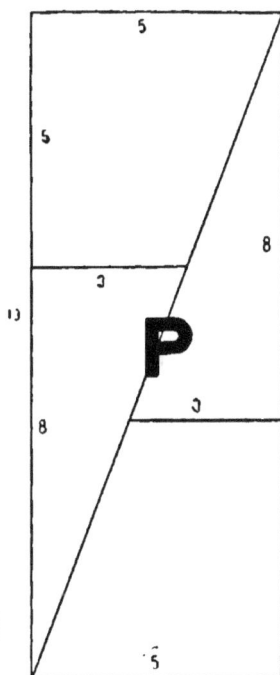

$$8 \times 8 = 64 = 10 = ⊕$$
$$5 \times 13 = 65 = 11 = \times + ⊕ = ⊠$$

$$5 \times 13 = 65 = 1 = \times$$

	1
01	29
⊕	×

	2
01	29
01	11 = ⑩

12	90
3	90 = 12	0

$$3 \quad 0 = ⑩$$

---

[1]   × on ⊕ is the turtle.

[2] 129. $1 + 2 = 3$. $3 + 9 = 12$ end L. It will be seen that the T square is the salvation by ||| the trinity — 3 sticks — T and the pen.

The result, is the cruise I fix on.

Mill, is M ill = 13 sick.

Cents, is sent S, sense. S = 19 = ☉.

See Fig. 13.

The law of four, is the law of the cross. For this reason the German says *fear* for four, and one on dread, for one hundred.

The difference in time of the almanac man's head being in Aquarius, and in Aries, is seen to be two months. There are twelve signs in the northern heavens that propel the twelve signs of the zodiac in the southern or middle heavens, and, as the distance is great, the signs do not work exactly opposite; there is a twist of two months time between them. So, finally, this man is off of the southern[1] zodiac and lives in the twist.

The southern zodiac no longer controls him because the power is always from the north. This is the difference between the sun and the north, and the difference between the A and O.

Because of this. two months' twist, it requires the same time for Mercury to reach this earth; the exact time is sixty-six days. $6 + 6 = 12 =$ L the right angle. He comes on the square, and here is where both ends meet, and why a worm which puts both ends together is an angle-worm. The word angel is from angle, and is of the same letters.

The signs in the north revolve faster than their counterparts in the south, and thus make the principle of the gain twist.

---

[1] In *southern*, see time oh you *th* he are N = 14 = 5 = ☐ = law.

CHAPTER XVIII.

Nineteen centuries of time, set on the first 19 letters of the Roman alphabet as now arranged. The first is A a, the second is A b, the third is A c, the fourth is A d, and so on through to the nineteenth, which is now A s. In this way, syllables and their connections have determined the history of the world.

The inward man is constructed on this law of division by 19, in the distance between, and the connections of, the digestive organs.

See rector, wreck tom, die wreck ton, directon,[1] wrecked on, wreck D on, wrecked ham, E wrecked ham, wrecked you M, wrecked hum, rectum — the end of digest and the law.

W, is 4 sticks — 2 right angles and the cross where all double.[2]

V is also a right angle, but the same as W is acute in print to show good spacing.

At the year 1901, the sphyncter and sphynx of time will be reached, which will be the letter T. Those two sticks of T are put on the letter P to make the monogram of Pan = P.[3]

In that monogram is D and 3 sticks to build with. The eye is always allowed with one stick. Thus of P can be built D I T, D I X, and so on. This is puny, and punny; the puerile way.[4]

The word juvenile, is Jew ✓ Nile; the same as baby square on = Babylon. Nile, is line — the plumb of the raven rout from the eye at the hub of the firmament; the dove finds no rest for the sole[5] of its foot and returns to the ark — arc.

The Carthagenian language was Punic. It is the strongest

---

[1] Die and *re* on † is in the word direction. To *re*, is to change from a soul to a spirit and live again.

[2] Every individual must take the W to himself, as double I. Those are the same four sticks of M = 13 = 4. M and W unite in *mow*, *maw* and marrow, by the sentence M are ah (R) O double you; see it is the M arrow = the sun ray.

[3] History reads, that "Constantine placed bones on the letter P," but gives no reason.

[4] In puerile, is the purr of the throat, the lie = lye, and the law = ▢.

[5] Soul.

language man can use. He does use it continually; but his dulness of comprehension, and his ignorance of where to place syllables in the outer court of the temple, lead him to see weakness and folly in a pun.

The understanding of the double read is earthly wisdom; the understanding of double read doubled, is heavenly wisdom.

The letter T, is the cross at the apex of the temple of time, (Fig. 12) and is with A, the syllable At — the twentieth century. Every division of time known to man is to be divided by 20 in the law. Moses died at one on dread and T went Y — 120, and the story of Joshua is of the same division.

At the close of the 20th century, the 2000th year whirl will be whirled off, and will have been a world of time. The O (naught) is with D (od — do) in world, and the eye is in whirl with H allowed — hallowed.

In *world*, is 4 sticks, double U U (the two are the orbit of the earth) and Lord.

When people of this age presume that the ancients were low down in the superstitious folly of paganism, they are assuming to know the law of God as they in their own minds frame it for him. They seem to consider the law of God as something foreign to this earth, which will not apply to their guilty souls until they have forgiven themselves in a court of their own convening. They seek for a religion in which there is no punishment to be considered.

There is no greater mistake for man. Pun is meant, the pun *ish* I H S meant, pun is H meant, the suspension in the great H the now silent space over head. There will the soul learn the double reed, and the double *read*, and will say sifolish, after shiboleth. The "*ish*" of the Jew, is *his* I H S.

In the figures 1900, draw a line downward between the **19** and the 2 ciphers; then a cross line underneath, making a T square inverted; then add the 1 and 9 together, which makes 10; place this amount under the 19, then bring down the 2 ciphers below the line, and see the 1000 years that "Satan shall be bound; after that he shall be loosed for a season."[1]

---

[1] See page 276.

Here is the Unicorn with the chain around the belly let loose; the pike in the fore — 4 — head, is the pen and the spear of Mars, *God of War.*

1900 years here on this earthly ball, is just 1000 years in some other sphere of God's temple; and just as mystical as this process of figuring is, just so mystical is every tale in the biblical mythology of the history of the earth and its productions.

After the A t century, the year *one* will commence again, and will be the first of another 1900 years — the double A again.

CHAPTER XIX.

THE messenger Mercury comes to this earth in the 1886th year, counting from the double A, the year after the cross at the apex is completed.   See Fig. 12.

The body which is to receive this spirit, is born in the sign Virgin, the 12th day — death.   13 is death unto a new life by the sun, so on that night between life and death, does the child's life quiver in the balance.

The wood type of the birth is poplar; the same of the second life, is elm — he square M = 13 the sun.   In poplar, is ♇ and polar.

AN ANCIENT ALPHABET.

He.	Shing.	Whang.
Ho.	Phon.	Br.
Sef.	Fen.	Yah.
Nigh.	O.	I.
Shag.	Koko.	Els.
Sou.[1]	Confo.	
Lig.	Po Yo.	Tui.
Fo.		

This child is Ishmael; in which see I H S and the mahl and
weasel. His hand is against every man's, and every man's
against his. He is born to suffer in the flesh what souls must
suffer out of it. He is constructed in nature as facing the opposite way from all mankind. He is the H airy man Esau — he saw.
His brother took his heel and connected the circle of time. He

---

[1] Weasel, whezze all, el, L.

was red by the reed, read. Threescore is 3 T s and *th* re score — the time core in the throat of Esau and Jacob, the twins.

His make up in numbers is as

$$135 = \quad 9 = \text{eye.}$$
$$132 = \quad 6 = \text{Virgin.}$$
$$\overline{267 = 15 = \text{God.}}$$

The make up of all other people is as

$135 =$	9	267
$123 =$	6	258
$\overline{258 = 15}$		$\overline{9}$

The difference is the eye, although the same figures are used.

In all Bible stories which give seven, it is to be multiplied by itself. Here rest on the seventh as one and octave, two and octave, three and octave, four and octave, five and octave, six and octave, seven and octave; the octave has swallowed itself, and the moon sun[1] man dies the ash death at the age of forty-nine.

He is the Phœnix[2] who springs from the ashes and lives in flames — F square hames the garrote of the bull.

His previous year was forty-eight,

$$4 + 8 = 12 \text{ death and L.}$$
$$4 + 9 = 13 = \text{M the sun as 13;}$$

the gateway to the silent Ⱨ, as A is the D sun, and H is the connection between G and A by the gamut, the law of seven upon which one rests to complete the temple — 8.

His birth is in 1836;[3] use the T square and see the result.

$$18 \mid 36$$
$$9 + 9 = 18, 1 + 8 = 9 \text{ the eye.}$$

9 is 7 and 2; the unity and the holy number.

The octave dies at seven, and is renewed by adding one for the temple and a foundation for its repetition.[4]

---

[1] Origin of monsoon.　　　　[2] Salamander.
[3] Calling 2001 the first year.　　[4] Reap he tit eye on.

See O, co means life, and oc means death; oc with the key added, means death unto life; the syllable is ock; u c k is the same for the soul. Co means life with death in the distance, as O is to be gone through to see God. Oh see C with the drawbridge of salvation, the reed (read) which shows C to be G at that time.

G, is seven, and that seven is serpent even strict time and its consequences. Even, is he V he N = V is N; N has the reed, and thus [1] is M = 13 = sun. V has the rod and is N.

The observance of calendar days was brought about by the knowledge of the course of the cruise through the year of trans-formation.

Purgatory is connected with the outskirts of hell.

The Divinity, is the existence of God the Father with God the Virgin — the holy mother all in one.

The Trinity, is the same God the Father, the Son, and the Holy Ghost.

As every word has four meanings, man on earth cannot have a clear perception of the divination.

The Holy Ghost is the presence of God's influence throughout all space, the way he reaches every one. With the fleshy eyes, the little gaseous threads of the Holy Ghost cannot be seen.

In this way, God controls all things. He fights all sides in war, and causes all disasters [2] and desolation.

These things are all done on time, and by the law of the astronomical alphabet and its numerals. When mankind realize this, they will understand the epoch of time in which they live.

---

[1] *th* U S.   [2] D as Tar.   D is a star — disaster.

CHAPTER XX.

MERCURY pierced the Easter-egg. The earth is the yolk, and the air is the white of that egg. He comes in '86; add these figures and see 14 = N his number on high. He finishes [1] the course in '87; which add and see 15 = O. Then there is left 13 years on the A and S century, his number [2] on earth, the M.

$$86 + 87 = 173 = \quad \underline{01 \mid 73}$$
$$\oplus \quad \oplus \qquad \text{See Fig. 7.}$$

1901 is the year in which the firmament commences to cross the serpentine orbit at the apex as shown in Fig. 12. It is in shape like the central part of Fig. 14.

It is hung in the center, and swings around as it moves along on the 8. In the divisions of time on the 8, lays the law Hebraic.

The year 1888 is, by Roman [3] indication, the year one; see the 8 three times in that number. See A T (cat) the 20th century.

$$\underline{18 \mid 88}$$
$$9 \quad 16 = 7 = \text{G.}$$

The whole firmament turns around once in passing over one half of the 8, on its own axis, and is at the same time turning in a crosswise direction to its axis at the same rate of speed; turning one way and rolling the other way as it travels along on the doubled 8.

Here are all of the mathematical laws combined in this and the continued course of the serpentine orbit.

---

[1] Finish is $\dashv$ in *ish* = I H S. = ⨸ is finished, when the weakest becomes the strongest.

[2] Number, is N becomes M and $\oplus$.

[3] The roe man.

Fig. 12 is the course of that orbit. The space enclosed in the center is not a square, but the rhombus, from which is the word rhomboid, etc. As there are double tracks at the crossing, the

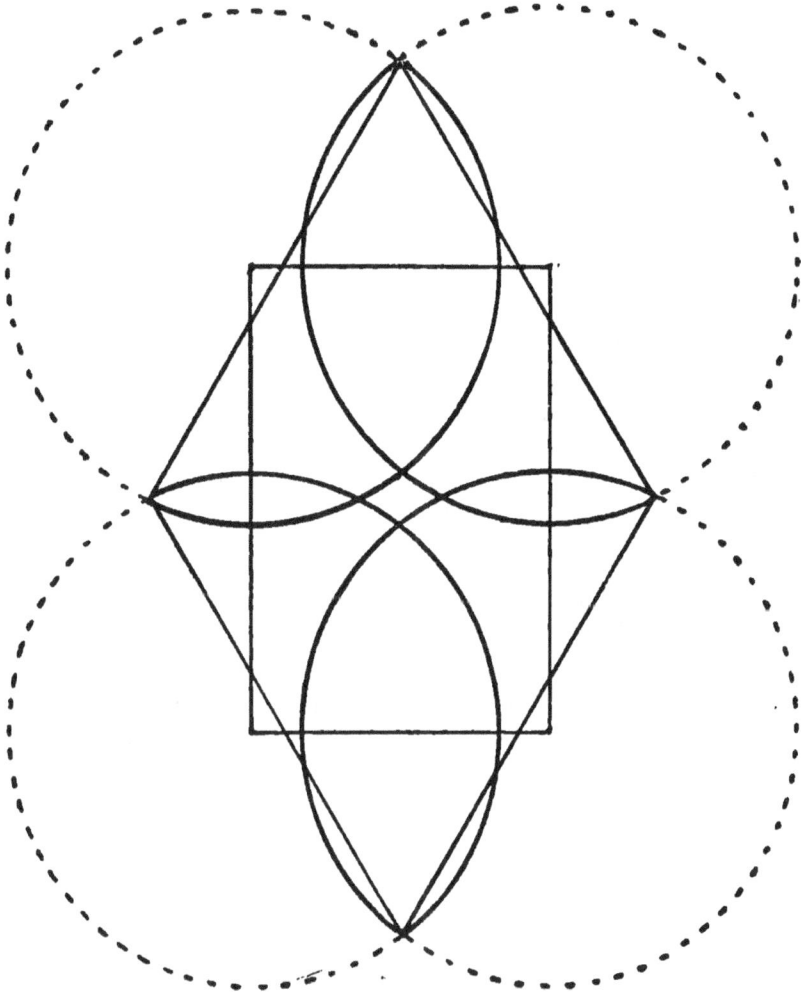

Fig. 14.

course is traced over the 2d time, and the 3d, and so on forever; first to the left,[1] then to the right. This course is the track that the whole firmament is following along on, and is *the* serpent.

---

[1] Left foot first — death at the easterly cross, the Ram.

Now, take a medium size cord, and coil it in this same double-track 8 shape, beginning on the ground and lapping one 8 directly on top of the one beneath it, until 24 have been formed; then take a wire and pass it down through the hole in the center, and bend the wire into a hoop, fastening the ends together with the cord strung on, and see the shape of the track of the firmament, and the construction of the great serpent of time — the writhe of the python.

Fig. 14 is drawn with 4 segmentary lines and shows the firmament.

Mark out an oblong square 6 by 9; then at a radius of 5, draw 4 circles, using the 4 corners of the oblong for centers. Two lines drawn through the center at right angles will measure 10 by 17. See in these figures the principle of time. (Draw 4 circles without a center space and the law of chaos is seen.)

17 is $1 + 7 = 8$ the H $=$ temple.

10 is $1 + 0 = \oplus$.

6 by 9, is $6 \times 9 = 54$. $5 + 4 = 9$, the eye, and $5 \times 4 = 20 = \mathsf{T} = + = \mathsf{W}$.

The 4 circles make 2 longitudinal hoops, the equatorial and the ecliptical circles also. The radius of 5 is the law of the weasel — the hole of the whole. The north pole line is the gate to heaven; the south pole is the blow-hole for chaff — see haff, half. Half, is alpha — when F becomes P — $\wp$.

If the 4 sides of the rhomb are multiplied, the result is 100; 10 of which is $\oplus$; the O which is left, is the she goat, and the pen with it is the he goat $10 = \oplus$. $\oplus$.

Thus it is seen that God's temple has an actual existence in space, and is the perfect law of mathematical principles.

Man has to be adjusted to the law as he goes along in progression. It is a reality, and material, just the same as things on the surface of this earth are. His spirit goes to another planet, to a new body, where things are much more harmonious than on this earth, and so on in progression to eternal life.

The souls of men are the seed of Abraham. The seed leaves the body, is purified and replanted in a body so exquisite that man's comprehension fails in the effort to realize it. The coming of the spirit to the body of a man here, is a type of spirits leaving this earth for the joys of immortality; but God is perfect, and those seeds must be good in order to take root and pass along.

Now return to Fig. 12 — the track with the rhombus in the center. Call the lower circle 1, the upper circle 2, and the center space 3. Add together 1, 2, and 3, and see 6. The firmament must pass over this track twice to complete the Temple of time; namely, 8000 years. By the passing around these 3 spaces 1, 2, and 3 twice, the law of 12 is established,[1] and is death to that cycle of time, the end of the world-whirl D.

The firmament in travelling on the track of this serpent — 8, — turns over on its axis once in the bottom half, and once in the top half; and, at the same time, turns crosswise of its axis once in the bottom half, and once in the top half, establishing the law of quadrature in the heavens.

The turning over 4 times in completing this cycle of time is to be multiplied by 4, because of the two halves of the 8 being passed around twice each; so $4 \times 4 = 16$, and this is the same 16 — the arch.

It requires 1900 years of time to pass over one half of the 8, and near the close of that time — just 14 years previous — does the law come back to earth by the messenger Mercury; 14 years brings up to the rhombus, then 100 years — for crossing the rhombus — completes a circle of time.

Once over the course by the left-hand track is a 4000 year cycle of time. Another course over the right-hand track is a 4000 year cycle the same; the two are a great cycle of time and the temple — the octave — the rest on the seventh.

The firmament is travelling on a track which is itself travelling on another track of just the same form, but much larger. The first track is 16; the course of the 16 track is the 32 track, the course of the 32 track is the 64 track. All of these tracks are turning, each and all of them separately, on the line of their axis,

---

[1] For established, read

"he ✠ a Ⓓ square *ish* he died.
He stab square I H S he ☾ .
Est alibi she (the womb man) ☾ .
I stable shed.
Each of the fore (4) going can be read four ways $= 16 = 7 = G$.

and crosswise at the same time ; [1] add together the 64 — the last
and largest track, and see $6 + 4 = 10 = \oplus$.   The straight
mark is the upright in the letter B, and the O is the 2 half circles
in the same letter.   See that they are 2 D D s, and that it is the
same law that divides the bean, and the pea, and that it takes
the 2 halves to make a whole and perfect seed = see D.   The
sprout is the S $\wp$ rout.

Observe that the figures 64 are both even ; and that 6 is the
virgin, and ♃ the sign of Jupiter, Jove, Janus.   Here see why
$\oplus$ is a hieroglyph meaning God, as seen in Fig. 7. 10 = B =
$\oplus$. $\oplus$.

Outside of all globes is the principle of $64 \times 2 = 120$, where
no solid earthly matter exists.   There is the inside layer of the
double tire.   Outside of that layer, is the principle of 120×2
$= 240$ — the outside layer which completes the double tire, and
the two are the *tyre.* Tyre has the Y in it, the 25th letter. $2 + 5$
$= 7$.   By the law it requires two Y Y s to make an I.[2]

$Y = 25 = 7$. $YY = 14$. $YY = 50 =$ the law and O.   In
this way the temple of time is built for the Jews, and the way
it has always been done since man inhabited the earth.

Z is lightning in the law, and is the power of the whole 25 together.   It is the 26th ; $2 + 6 = 8$ — the temple.

Castor leaves heaven as N, and arrives on earth as Mercury ;
he takes the pen from the left side of M which leaves the diagonal line of N in a crosswise position ; this erects the suffering
cross.   It is the same line through $\wp$.

By taking the pen from M, N is left — the leaven which
leaventh the whole — leave N.   That yeast was Y cast, Aries,
the last of Pisces — the leap in the dark.

By taking the pen, tom becomes ton ; T on = on the cross.
Here is the *rock,* the ℞ ock (uck) the foundation of the church.

Ch UR see H, church.   Ch is K, and in the word church, are
these two ch keys, and the *ur* in the center is UR of the Chaldees = see all D D s = Ⰽall ☽ Ds = $\oplus\oplus$.

---

[1] The word *add,* is the sun and the same 2 D D s = $\oplus$.

[2] Two Y Y s become 2 ⋀ ⋀ s which is a 24 hour circle of light on the earth, and
an eye on the mill from the north, sees the ⋀ ⋀ s as W and X; Ours — Hours 24.
$2 + 4 = 6$, 6 marks in W and X.

In tottle, see the Ts of Golgotha. Tottle in Aries, is Aristotle; so a man by that name was a philosopher. Phil O so; Phillip who died with his face on the pillar — the od column = ⊂. He rode Pegasus, and was hurled into the Styx.

Mankind have a difficulty in placing many of these sayings, because they took place both in body and spirit. To think of them as having taken place in space and in spiritual life, is to excite the imagination beyond its soul power.

The curtain is drawn to all mankind, and only *one* ever comes back from behind the scenes to the *foot* light with a ℙ laws = applause — the En hakkore.

Eagle.	Cuckoo.	Weasel
Ossi-frage.	Little & Great Owl.	Chame-leon.
Osprey.	Stork & Heron.	Ferret.
Vul-ture.	Lapwing.	Lizard.
Raven.	Bat.	Tor-toise.
Owl.	Locust.	Mouse.
Night-hawk.	Beetle.	Snail.
	Grass-hopper.	Carcass.

CHAPTER XXI.

Every syllable in language has 4 meanings. They are all connected together by the inward nature of the resemblances of themselves in those 4 meanings. They have meanings which connect the earthly with the heavenly. They all blend softly together, and the things which they describe all have some similarity in earth and heaven.

Two meanings are all that man can expect on this earth. The *ish* of the Jew, is also *his:* but when put together as I H S,[1] the articulation is lost to man, but not to heaven. So it is with all syllables. The word *describe*, is the scribe after death ; the *des*, is the death and time after, and *scribe*, is the time crib and weasel.

The foundation is to sound every letter with the whole 7 vowels; commencing A with B, *i.e.* 1 with 2, 2, then 3 on with 2, 1 with 3, and so on through the 25 letters by the law of chances in displacement, until the last possible combination is taken ; this is the law of quadrature in sounds.

When the soul leaves the body, it will see 4 meanings to every act and circumstance and combination of circumstances, with a focus on everything at once according to the law of quadrature. The 4 quarters of the heavens gathered up as in a scroll.

How to "read B ": b read bread from the kingdom of heaven :[2] done by the man A, the manna, and in *this*[3] manner it has always been done.

In the law of four, a moon — *th*, man — *th*, month, is composed of four octaves (weeks), and is ruled by the moon : $4 \times 7 = 28 = \odot$. To this 28 days add 1 to make the last octave, giving 29 days ; this is the law of 29, so easy to see in the physical construction of both sexes.

---

[1] The highs — Fig. 7.
[2] B re ad. B he a D — bead. B ad D bad.
[3] *This* is the superscription.

Two and nine, are eleven = 11 = unity, the X: the union with God and man, is by subtracting, 11 = 2, *i.e.* the marks of eleven are 2; subtract 2 from 11 leaves 9 the eye.[1] That eye on man is the connection. Eleven, is he square even.

A man's life in a month is less than a twelfth of 365 days, *i.e.*, the circle from toes to head made 12 times, is by the moon's time.[2] When his functions are stretched out and off of moon time by the sun, his body dies. His functions become punctions of the soul. That soul sees puns immediately. Its past life all comes back with a double meaning. To live is to doubt it, and to die is to know it. *It,* is the eye and † = ☦ .

When a body dies, it gets first on to a level with the moon's time, then on to the sun's time and course.[3] Here is the moon turned to blood, and the sun gives no light. Light becomes ghilt.

All souls[4] must experience these things before they can become vitalized spirits. He who suffers these in soul and body is Diana; died by the moon, and entered the temple with the sun.

The functions of man are stretched beyond the moon's time by the sun's influence, and passed from the law of four on to the law of twelve and a half[5] at death, and his soul goes to purgatory, the great matrix — the zodiac in which he was first moulded and held in place by the moon's time and influence.

In Fig. 15 is the law of larvæ. The soul lays dormant (T ☾ for four months, while four signs pass. Every little thing of his life comes back in his purgatorial dreams. He sees no end to

---

[1] The letters of cat are 3, 1, 20, which add, and see 24 = 6, the virgin. This is why 6 is 9 re versed. The re verse, is because of seeing in all directions. 9 and 6 added, is 15 = O, the club added is 01 = ☽. This club is the three-leaved clover = see square o V her = he *are*, see lover. Leave ☾ = leaved, leave L = level, leave N = he leaven = eleven = II, leave R = liver, the pin from R out = the rout of I = one = oh knee = the goat. See the four-leaved clover of Aaron = green = G neer = near, the Æ.

[2] Less than a year by the sun.

[3] Goes to the cross of the Styx — T X I — X I T.

[4] Souls, soles, feet, Pisces, the *last.*

[5] The nine pen see ninepence.

rhymes in the story of his life. From larvæ, he becomes a laugher = square halfer, then off ℞ and off he goes.

He was of the house of Levi = evil; as Levi, he was cast into hades where ◖ becomes T, so dormant turned to torment.

In dormant is dor, the foundation for dor bug: he who is searching for light in darkness.

The soul goes in to the come oh toes state, because he went by fire from the toes to that state. State is ⚕ ate: he ate of the fruit on the cross, and became a ☉ liver. Levi and ℞, is in liver.

CHAPTER XXII.

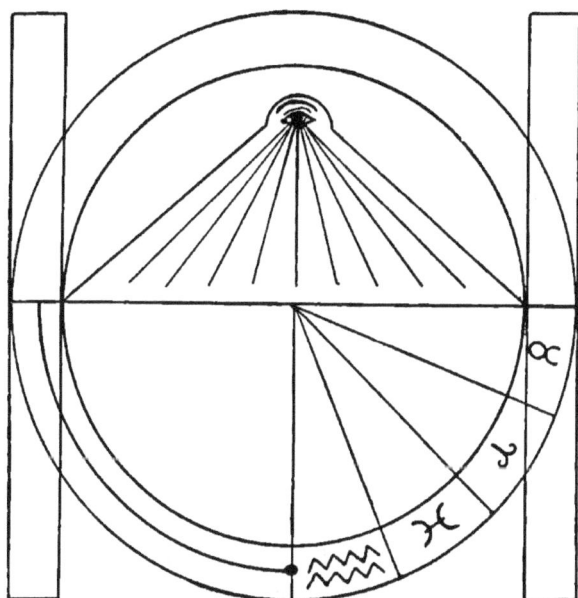

Fig. 15.

Gallows on which Haman was hung.

HADES, hay tis, hat is, high tis, H eye tis — hight is, height is, 8 is, ate is the fruit of the tree, and the soul goes marching[1] on. The words of this earth are stumbling-blocks to a soul; it has to Hebrew the whole before it is a spirit perfect.

The simplicity of the work is astonishing when one once gets the meaning of syllables as applied to a soul on its path after it leaves the body.

The word *said* becomes sad, because the eye (I) is on the soul. *Meant,* becomes ment, for the reason that the soul is in

---

[1] March in G, pass in Aries, the left first.

the sun (A), and as that soul goes on, it sees all without the study of stumbling-blocks.

The *harp* is the seeing with a circular focus the four quarters of the heavens at once, with a perfect knowledge of the four meanings of language.

All language is the same music founded in the heavens, and used on earth as a resemblance which everything bears to a spiritual existence. It has a solid connection with earth by way of the sun man's history; in which look for an explanation and application of all syllables and letters.

Perfect, is ℘ he are, ғ he see T, = ℙ is ℞, and F see the cross. In that word, see *re* feet.

In man, see M is N, and N is M with A = the sun; by leaven, M is N = ʹN a N with the reed = nan Y the goat.

Man is made in God's image, split in two, male and female; disjointed, as compared to the image of God. They are all on the od number of 3, the letter C as shown in Fig. 1. They are all travelling toward the 4th — the letter D — the even number on which they all die.[1] The half moon does it for every monthly number who are called home to God. It is an impossibility for man to feel the even numbers, or the even and odd together — the chromatic column under the letter G in Fig. 3.

The D and od numbers are the devil; no power can withstand them (him). God handles men by the use of this od column. It is the brad of the gourd[2] with which he drives man to all his acts. To discover it, is to die.

Discover, is D is cover; every thing hid by that D.

God is the principle of a male and female united together in one solid body, and that body doubled — making the four. This is the head centre of four ways to everything, and why the figure ♃ is the sign for Jupiter.

The northern half of the firmament, which extends beyond the pole hub, is the farther side from this direction on earth; so there is correctly God the Father. The influence *that* way, is

---

[1] They die on a ☽ turned to the right. They must get (☾) one turned to the left to put with it, making a ☾ — the in balance.

[2] G O you are death ☽ ah a death brad.

the male influence, and *this* earthly way, the female influence, is the Virgin.

Virgin is the word given in the law, and is the power of those letter characters.

Ate, eat, reate, *re* eat, see *re* eate — create. Eat ⊋ , the taste of death and *re* created. Re created every 8000 years, and the fruit eaten every 2000 years, and re creating at every such time.

The Holy Ghost is of material. It is extremely fine gaseous H air all through God's kingdom. It is in the air in which man lives, and it controls him in all his acts. When man is penitent he draws sympathy from this source. The mystery of this can never be known while the soul is in the body.

The touch of this hair to the soul singes the gaseous envelope surrounding it, and causes the sulphur like scent of the ⊕ ℞ ☛ Ⱶ ⊠ ☐ which is the Hebrew for brimstone.[1]

The virtue of a person on earth should be as strong as the dread of that voyage through a whirlwind of unearthly fire where the seed is taken out of the husk.

This invisible hair is the northern light phenomena which can sometimes be seen through the murky atmosphere at a great distance, and in the direction from which it comes.

In this fineness is three kinds. The G, the O, and the D. D is the devil, and all in the word God. If man had the cycloptic eye of a spirit for one second of time, he would fail to the earth in utter humiliation. He would see the same ⊠ ℞ *th* (D) lights all around in doors and out, and see just how he is hitched to his fate. F ate as ℘ , and knows it. Nose, is *no see;*[2] knows, is K now S. See why knew is new. Know becomes knew. It is the key to the bottomless P eye T[3] that unlocks the gates of hell.

Syllable, is from see L a bull;[4] every syllable sound that man can utter is founded upon this same law.

Bell means the church; bel and ble are the same tailed out.

---

[1] The soul sees and smells this when in sheol; the D part — depart into hades, the home of the damned.

[2] Smell M, no see M.

[3] ℘ ☛ † — Pit.

[4] The soul ill in sign Taurus.

The word *slay* is the time lay — destruction by time. As one sign of the heavens succeeds another, it is said to slay the one which precedes it. So the Ram attacks the bull, but always in the character of Orion.

Orion takes on the name of the Ram, and so on through the 12 signs. This is the same course which every soul takes in purification, as it is successively drawn under the signs which compose the heavenly matrix.

These principles were understood (they knew that they stood under them) away back in the mists of antiquity; and in and on those temples, now in ruins, they did inscribe praise to God.

That part of architecture was named the frieze, because of the cold direction from which the law came. The Z roe is the same cold suffering. *Cold,* is see O square death; see *old:* see old D, cl is the same as all. See old man, becomes see ol D man, and cold man becomes cole man, He who "heaps coals of fire on the heads of unbelievers." He is the "double," and of course the *plural* man. Plural is ℘ square you are all, for one way of reading, and there is no way of getting away from the law of the plural.

Among the tales of the Bible is that of the three sons of Noah. It is a very subtile[1] tale. God was no ℞[2]. His three sons were 3 divisions in the life of Pan.

For 49 years he was Shem.[3] He went into fire, and was Ham.[4] From this is the name of smoked thigh — *th* eye. Grease for cold regions, and grace for cold death, all in the blend of heavenly with earthly facts.

A people, by a very close form of worship, once said that they were unworthy to eat of smoked pork: others said it was all

---

[1] Low — deep — hard to fathom.

[2] Noah.

[3] Shame.

[4] By seeing his "Father's nakedness," is meant, that he saw God while his soul was caught up from earth. As Shem, he could not see him, for he had not yet died. As Japheth, he could not, for his spirit was back in the flesh. He and his brothers were all the same man in that riddle. He was Ham while he was going through the fiery furnace of the transfiguration. In the two other divisions of his life the mantle was spread. He could not see God through his eyes of flesh and blood. In *this* is the foundation for what men may do in the law of resemblances on earth.

gammon.[1] The word fits, because Ham was on the G Ham on. After the triumph over death, Ham became Japheth. J a ph he *th* — J a P *th*.

Those who wrote biblical stories, and a great many more of the same kind, knew the *facts* to begin with ; they then could write riddles in which were to be found some part of the life of him who was known to be the man of his time.

All could not read, but those mythical tales could be told from mouth to ear for generations, and people believed them, as all having taken place on earth ; the same as is forever natural to those who have not yet suffered death.

This has been God's way of doing it. It has always fitted the times, and has been the means of salvation for those who could not read the double reeds of Pan.

In the flood myth (mith), Noah is God ; the family of eight is his arch — ark — the H.[2] The 150 days, is the law of O the 15th, through which all go to the rivers that water Eden — the destruction of all flesh.[3]

The Tower of Babel is a myth which fits the explanation of the double reed of Pan every 2000 years, and has always held good.

In the myth of Elisha bringing the child to life, see Shunammite a shoe man mighty. That child sneezed *seven* times — the G styx. Sneezed, is time, knee, (by) Z he died. K goes with nee, because the key is with the ne Pan — the goat N he.[4]

The word myth is the *four truth.* It is my *th* (fire), and comes from JEHOVAH.

---

[1] Abomination. Hum bug. ⊙ you G.

[2] Whatever the destruction on earth, the animal life is always replaced by twos—male and female ; and by *sevens*, the law upon which all rests. In this way they enter the arc = the segment of the whole, as by their vision they know of nothing more ; but in *vision*, the eye is on, and there is the virgin eye and sion.

A certain combination of signs will cause the extinction of some animal life for a period of time ; but that life will be *re* created again and again, by twos, and the law of sevens ; see salvation in the arc, arch, ark, hark.

[3] D is the bow in the clouds = one death D eat H.

[4] M and N are seven sticks = G.

CHAPTER XXIII.

PAN was a pagan 2000 years ago, the same as forever. The Romans, in their ignorance, could not make a connection with him, because they compared his knowledge to their ignorance.

The carpenter, car painter — chariot painter[1] of Aleppo, was a black man, and not to be listened to.[2] The fate of that empire was sealed, and God hardened their hearts with the D, the same as he did the hearts of the Egyptians 4000 years before that advent.

The twelve gods of 8000 years ago, the 12 tribes of Israel[3] (eye is real), the 12 sons of Jacob, the 12 gods of Greece, the 3 and 9 muses of the Egyptians,[4] the 12 apostles, and all tales of the 12 in the law of God are the same ; the covenant has never been changed. Paganism was, and *is*, Christism and Christianity.

Paganism was not the cause of the sins of those days, nor is Christianity the cause of the sins of the present time.

When this man is born into a race of people, that race become the Jews, — the chosen for the next 2000 years following, — and all the rest of the earth become the Gentiles for the same length of time.

2000 years ago this man was a Carthagenian, and a black man ; that race have been the Jews for the past circle of time, and their redemption came as promised in holy writ.

In Abraham, find Bramah. In Lincoln is much when put upon the altar. See the missing link found. L in C[5] oh L N and colon. A colon is two dots $=$ D ots. The dot doubled, is $\oplus$ ot, the boot, the foot of God on his stool the $\smile\!\!^!$ — the 10th.

---

[1] Char painter.

[2] He worked on wood and painting — the building of chariots for the hippodrome.

[3] His ray L.

[4] M you see, muse. Mew see the whine — wine of the *kat*. It is amusing — a muse in G, to use M use; muse on 13 and stupidity, st you $\wp$ high dity.

[5] In the read of the red sea $=$ see A.

The 15th amendment was O, the 15th letter, and Ham end meant.

In Booth, see boot and *th* connected by and at the T = †, also boot and the ††. This calls to mind the play, our American cousin = see O you sin, see O us in.

In all of God's work there are forewarnings and echoes. These echoes are his approval and seal. The slave Burns (fire) of fugitive slave law fame was a warning. The raid at Harper's Ferry was another. Fort Sumter fired on in Taurus the 12th (death) was a distinct mark of the almighty arm of God. See, in the early history of that war, the dates and the frequency of battles which began with B, also the names of commanders.

Big Bethel, Balls Bluff, Baltimore,[1] Bull Run and the stone B ridge, are the leading ones for battles, and the whole lay is easily seen by those who see the read of C, the natural key in music, the red color of the Red Sea.

Lee means destruction, as see a "lee shore;" spell by the reverse and see *eel*, which means life. The double E refers to him who slew the lion of July.

In the word Davis is time and David. Day vis — V *is*. Day vision. Die — vision; division. By death vis-a-vis. The visor (D visor) of hell met — helmet. D and Siva.

That war was the direct language of God to man; the same as the Angel of the Lord slaying thousands with the sword — the S word — the time word — wor D — war D; one of the wards in the lock of the L ock — death unto knowledge.

Between the spelling of words there is a soft blend to be seen in pronunciation: Him, hymn. The Y and soft H see; the urn and the mysteries in the great H, the silent temple of God.

The 12 principal cities of the South were taken. This epoch of time was known by the ancients, as the "battle of the gods."

See the names of generals all through the war of the re bell eye on; the siege of Petersburg, Fort hell, and every circumstance by name and date.

Ulysses (July sees) is well known to be Pan.

Twenty-five years after fire on Sumter, there came earth-

---

[1] L add and White knee Low L. Ladd and Whitney, Lowell, Mass.

quakes at the same place.   25 is a quarter and a right angle;
all done on the square.   The boomerang returned to the same
place to say I am God and there is no other.[1]

Adam (add Ham) was formed of the dust $=$ ◖ you $ of the
earth.   The sign Gemini was brought to a focus on this earth
in connection with other signs by the will and power of God.
Adam lived, suffered the cruise, lived his second life, and died.

Every 2000th year afterward, for five periods of time, did the
same thing take place, with the exception of a variation at the
6th time; when, with the sign of the Virgin added, twins were
created, man and woman, male and female, both sexes united
together with a membraneous formation which dried away, leaving them separate.

Adam was first (fire st $=$ *th* st) a black man because of the
heat of the earth $=$ he art, hart, tar $=$ Ararat.

Adam was one of several who were created at the first.   Each
succeeding batch were a shade lighter until the sixth, when he
and his twin were white.   They were the only ones formed at
that time, and from them came all of the white race.   " Adam "
was the name of the double man at those six periods of time.
Here is the work of the six D aye S (days), and the *re* st on the
seven *th*.

After a long time the earth became unfit for man.   It was then
shifted on its axis, convulsed, creating a new configuration and
more heat, and then another long period of cooling intervened
before a new creating of man.   This is the " spring time and har-
vest which shall never fail."

The M eat of Adam was locusts and wild honey.   Locust is O
see us T $=$ O see you $ by the leave L (level).   The humming
of the August locust is typical of the humming reed of G.

Wild, is double you eye square death.

Honey, is the H one Y — the hone that sharpens the razor.

Sweet, is time we he †, we set, double you double he †.

The girdle about his loins was the three starred belt $=$ bell †
of Hercules.   He prepared the way of the Lord by showing ♇
re paired, and made a twin.

---

[1] The boomerang is the square club.

See Hebrew from the brewery of bruin, the B ruin of the bear; the rate of see *re* ate create. The number of times of the heating and cooling of this earth is more than man can comprehend.

The meaning of marry is M airy — the airy sun. He who was aired (haired) in the sun, got a new wife. The single of W is L, which is of wife, *life*.[1] The first and last are the wives in mythological stories. He married the rib, of course, and was doubled.[2]

In Leah is heal, the H eel = the brazen serpent = $ = S T. Sarah is time and airy H. Sarai the rib. Rebekah is a call to rear[3] — R ear — A *re*.

The story of Job is all the same. His wife did not believe him to be immortal. She did not believe him to be other than himself or to know God, ot to know God, aught to know God, hot to know God, ought to know God, taught = taut to know God, naught to no God, naught Y.

The same was the wife of Samson. The wife in mythology is the first life of the man, as David. The second life is the child born in old age, and the rib, life doubled as wife by the LL; W[4] the cruise from 49 to 51.

Mythology is of four ways; way, is double you from A to Y the same.

Job is 10, 15, 2, = 27 = 9. J and Ob the serpent; observe serve Ob = ○ ① = 15 + 2 = 17 = 8.

The return of this epoch of time always brings many pests with it, for the reason of the return of the combination of signs which first gave life to many things on earth.[5]

This is what is meant by the plagues of Egypt. Their attention was called to it by the sun man Moses, but they said it was the combined result of nature, and that he knew not God. The darkness was the D ark, and felt, is fell T and elf.

---

[1] His first L life = wife.

[2] ① *ish* ○ P — Bishop, two ways, the twin.

[3] The rear is north in the temple.

[4] L was doubled on 4 points of the compass = the square (⌐8) cross.

[5] In carpet bug is arc and P E T; to slay the Lion, the bottom stick was taken from E, and that was the jaw of the Lion — the battle of July. Carpet, again, is see harp et = it. Apple-tree beetles and all pests are the result of this time. Pest = P est = P he $. See S and T centuries.

No one tale gives the whole life of the sun man, for it is impossible to bring in all the characters; in a spot here and there the most of it is given.

Paul was the same man; but, because of unbelief and persecution, he talked as though some other man was him. He was not allowed to explain the law to those who were frozen in their own imagination; but one can see, by his hints at the double meaning of things, that he was the sun man.

Those who have believed in an earthly king from heaven, should study well the old test A meant, and notice the pun *ish* meant of those who would not take any notice of the same man, because he did not come in a way of which they had prophesied.

The truth dawned on their minds when too late to repair the injury; then that peculiar people did mourn and long for that spirit to return again and save them.

They were willing to believe what *had been*, the same as people of to-day will extol a departed soul, while only the day before that departure they were cold and could see nothing in that man to praise. Such is the folly, weakness and indifference of man on his side of the moon.

When one of the Os in the word moon becomes A, he sees moan in place of moon.

M oh you are N — in G — mourning. "A soul has gone to its L on G home, and the mourners go about the streets." Man sees not his folly, because he has nothing to compare it with except the workings of the imagination. He sees the folly of others, and his comparison of that folly with his *desire* to avoid the *same*, is the extent of his disappreciation of such folly. This is why he does not openly condemn the wickedness of his kind. He would lose his popularity were he so to do.

Aristocracy. Aries talk racy. Talk comes from † o see. Oc, is the *last* sound in the throat of an expiring[1] body, and the syllable *dur* is the one that the lifeless body cannot utter; the soul meets it.

The words more and moore mean *eternal;* for there is always more time coming — the serpent forever.

---

[1] X pyre (fire) in G.

Aquarius and Pisces are the signs at the low quarter of man; see the names of all articles covering those parts. This quarter is the part of the circle where Peter sank in the lye ford of C, and the spirit Mercury came into his neck, so he triumphed over the ash death. He sank to the depth of the calf, but came to life and lived through Pisces, and as the Ram with the strength of Orion he met the bull in April. He walked the C in Pisces with the 2 feet — those fishes; *i e.*, so much of him was renewed.[1] The sun closed the circle from the toes to the head, instead of the moon's doing it.

Gar means the voice in the throat.[2] Gar is tar; *i.e.*, gar † he are.[3] The garter on the leg marks the depth of the sin K (sink) of Peter, sin co pay tie on (syncopation). Off of the usually accented note; got away from the *bar*. Sink is S in K; time in key.

The tale set to the name of Peter, fits the 12th bin[4] of the zodiac only; month Pisces. There has to be a new name story for all of the months of the year, and one for the whole; also stories for the year divided by 3, 4, 6, 8, 10, 12, and 20.

In Fig. 7 the globes are the bears and bars; the cross means the successful crossing of orbits, the opposite of chaos. See the habits and anatomy of bears; they suck claws = see laws. Their anatomy is an A tom Ƴ.

A globe is a verb, for it is never at rest. V he are B; see the V and ☉ as ♐, the goat of December.

Mankind knew these things in the past, and marked them in a multitude of ways; the understanding of which was their edu-

---

[1] This refers to his ending his life on C (Fig. 1). The cock crowing and the denial is to show that he was the man of the whole. Before the sun crossed the line of Arez and Liber he should deny him three times — the 3 of Golgotha. He was to die 3 times. ☾ nigh he ☽ denied. Peter was the cock, for he see ock — death and the key. In this way circumstances are connected with the temple of nature. He *wept* — W he ℗ T. Double you also, for he was ℗ T F † in sheol. By using many of the names to which Peter was entitled, the story can be reduced by many hundred thousand words less than it would be if the name Peter were used all through the tale. The Bible fits in heaven as it now reads.

[2] See gargle.

[3] Ter, Tar, Tæ ℞.

[4] Month.

cation, and was the way of making bricks with straw. If less than twenty-five letters were used, they put dots to mean the same.

They understood the blending of syllables, and knew what letters to double to make the twenty-five. They recognized the power that drove those twenty-five — the boomerang in the air.

No matter what syllable the work leads to, they all lead on and by, continuing on and on forever, always stopping at the I. Add S for time, and see *is.* The next is ⌘ and the club, which gives the whole.

In *that* see *th* and the sun and cross; this word is with hat as that † hat, that which is over head. Bonnet, is from *bone* and † ; the same is overhead.

These is *th* he see, by way of M = 13 as *th* he M them. This is the way Adam gave correct names to all things, and they were all brought to bear on his life; death, and a new life.

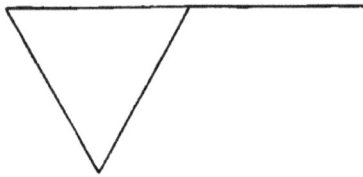

Adam's apron is the 4 sticks of his letter M, 3 of which form the lamb (triangle).[1]

The word forgive means 4 give, *i.e.*, give 4 — the letter D ;[2] because at death the life has been one D and the other ꟼ must be added to make the double D, which is seen to be the B written as ⌽. One ball bal once balance A, all from the scales of February, cold feet and the fete of D — the menu.[3]

Fig. 16.

Fig. 7 should be placed on the northern wall of the tabernacle, and a representation of the sun over the door of the southern wall, with a segmentary line drawn, to show the passing of the

[1] Eve's (Pollux) apron, was see L out — clout. Die appear again — the diaper, the cris-cross diamond.

[2] Also the four ways of the cross; D becomes T in the syllable *dit*; see C on dit — true time.

[3] The first life of Pan was a ꟼ turned to the left = east; his second life was a D turned to the right; together was ⌽. All mankind are the sheep; their lives here on earth are as D turned to the right = west. Their second D will be east, where and when they will suffer those same things which the soul of the man Ishmael did. Sheep on the right and goats on the left. Sheep will sleep, when H is L, as H he L; double L is double you, ꟼ O you ble, bell, bull to bear.

sun over the course of A, from east to west, see Fig. 17. This is the ark (arc) of the tabernacle of God.

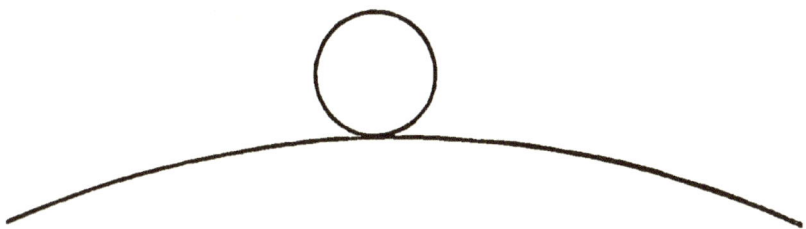

Fig. 17.

Southern wall of the tabernacle.

Only one person entered this at a time. He knelt, facing south, and repeated the following: Oh God, according to thy vengeance and thy tender mercies have compassion on me now and forever more. Selah.

The syllable *tude* (duct — dute) is chewed, when the II is with it as thude, in the soul's course. Longitude becomes long I chewed, L on G I chewed. It is the plumb line from the pole of the heavens to the arctic center; with latitude is the cross. D you wet.[1]

In the possible displacement of 25 letters lays the law that rules man in his daily rounds; because of his inability to unravel the combination, he does not discover the connected incidents of his life. Apply the double read to history, and see that God is existent, and that he rules with a "rod of iron."

Man has elevated himself above the art of punning, and considered it a sign of weakness and disability; and at the same time has piled up thousands of volumes of theology, in which the people could find no explanation of language which carried beyond the first reading, and after long lives of study and writing, those composers were at *last* only able to say, "God be

---

[1] Duett. = death you ate and became double — two parts — the twins.

merciful to me a sinner," as they took their final leave of those who were to read their works and follow after, repeating the same prayer in hope and faith, but knowing nothing of theology.

The back and forth of the sun from Cancer to Gaza, and the "see-saw" of the equinoxes, was the heavenly representation as shown to Adam. That is the square cross of a soul in sheol. The leap of the sun from the shortest to the longest day is one bar, the other bar is the line from east to west between the time of the sun crossing the line in spring and again in fall : spring being *east*, and fall *west*, in that law. *Longitude* plumb, and *latitude* level, is the course of adjustment.

See why the church did persecute those who first said that the earth revolved around the sun, instead of the sun around the earth.[1] The "grind of the mill" is just the same, which-ever way it fits the mind. Man has great difficulty in trying to comprehend the law of four ways to everything — namely the *square cross.*

The body and soul being adjusted to light and dark, — a split day, — the soul cannot leave this globe until it is adjusted to the circular parallels of latitude from 40 south, to the north pole, with the spray of longitude on the same circle from the north pole to the same 40th south latitude.

That mesh is M *ish.* It is the basket where the soul basks and asks $\odot$. It is the bush — $\odot$ ush L. This is adjusting a soul to 360 by 130.

These figures multiplied give 46800 = $\odot$ ate and two circles = lives. The spirit then leaves this globe by way of the pole line — the handle of the spinning top — T oh $\wp$.

The letter T shows a bit of longitude and latitude, and there in space, in sheol, the soul is readjusted = read just he died ; squared around A round, and as globular, leaves the suffering squares, "born again."[2]

---

[1] Man is given the temple as it fits the law of his vision. He suffers the re-adjustment as the law of his bodily organism fits inertia. Man's disposition to enforce his ideas on to others at the point of the sword, called down the ven-geance of God. He with the D evil did divide the church asunder, and brought misery, bloodshed and desolation on to this earth.

[2] Hebron = he born.

Thus the square is circled by way of the weasel; the piece is 8 (ate) and that spirit knows the tree of the knowledge of good and evil and of its fruit = F ah you *it* ♱.

By S S the spirit is double timed; twice 19 = 38 = 11 a twin, as X. In *twice*, see the icy way of T double you. Pure spirit cannot freeze.

The several expeditions toward the north pole should now be understood by names and circumstances.

Put glacier on the altar and see the wonderful things in dialect which can be found in the parts. See the O pen see C at the north pole = ℗ oh L he.

The *mesh* of longitude and latitude on which the soul is *lasted*, is the Meshach. The same is the Shadrach — the sh ad rack.[1]

The crib, the boy cot, the bed of suffering, the knee — (Pan) the 10th sign, is the A bed N he go — Abednego.[2]

The fourth was the sun man; all 4 *th* and so for*th*, for *th*, and so on all through the Bible, in what have seemed to be parts of a long story, can the same cruise be found. The spies sent to the land of Canaan was, of itself, a short story of the cruise of the twins. The reason why these all connect as long tales, is of the law of mathematics in letters. People could believe the stories as they read them, and there they had a foundation for religion and salvation. See the love of God.

---

[1] Bony shad rack.　　　[2] Bad he knee go = ℭ.

CHAPTER XXIV.

The sun man having suffered all the signs, from the moon south, through to the polar star north,[1] lives on the earth in the entanglement of eight times the cube of 25 letters, by the law of their possible displacement in the law of $75 = 12 = 3 + 1 = 4 \times 2 = 8$.

This gives the 4 quarters of the heavens above, and the same beneath. He takes the name Elias (alias) and all the names of earth will fit him.

Because of *his* suffering, many peculiar things will happen; many a catastrophe, and many a triumph. Many people will have hair-breadth (bread *th*) escapes, and recover from distressing ailments. See the slaying of the first-born.

The death of Ham, gives the history of deadham — Dedham. That bridge disaster was because of that leap from heaven to earth. See that the engine went over safe, the same as the one at White river.

See the water tank through that car at Bradford bridge on date Aquari the ⊕ *th*, and the name of the engine-driver. Driver, is *death river*.

Because of the ash death and the bridge on the letter C, the Ashtabula bridge disaster was, as a forewarning. Warning, is *war* N in G.[2]

Because of the turnover of ◖ , (D) is the history of Dover and Andover what has, and will be.

See 4 fires in New *Ham*pshire. Suncook, Lebanon, New Boston, Newton Junction — new ton and the junction with heaven earth and hell.

---

[1] ℗, as the little bear, is the F wrench = French. F ran see ☐ is France; thus understand N a pole leo ℗ O leon wars.

[2] In *war*, W is A and R; Ren, is a spirit; he builds in mort I see, the mortise hole in tim ⊕ he ℞ .

These are mentioned because easy to read. Those things which are more difficult to read, are none the less pointed.

"A priest after the order of Melchisedec forever," is the title that links together all Bible stories.

In *title*, is the lie (lye) and two crosses; he was forgiven on the last cross. *Forgiven* — 4 given; given 4 ways of understanding, and was that day with him in P ariy (airy) disc [1] the cub $\in$, the cube — 21 spots — U.

The 21 = 3. That 21 is *the* Abrasax, in which see a *brass ax*.[2]

Hero, is he of the ro, roe, row, of the zodiac; hence a row is a mob. Mob, is the M and O B the serpent.

All the signs in space have the form of some kinds of animal life, and by these signs is animal life produced and continued.

These signs all have a connection by the law of similarity in blending, and they are tied together by a network of electrical currents.

. As *this* man was drawn on to the influence of that sign which gave birth to worms and grubs, he chewed earth; when on to that sign which gave birth to spiders, he chewed flies; and so on through the whole course.

Job was the T man hight, and Bill dad the shew hight, the shoe eight from the 12 inch foot of Pisces. By Z he was fired Opher *th* air where the gold of that land is good. He was the Naaman height (name A *th* hite) also. In these three characters did Job talk with the Holy Ghost, to himself, to *his* ghost (Samuel), and within himself as the twin Castor and Pollux.

Mankind are all born (one excepted) under the sign Gemini, connected with the zodiac and signs Pegasus and Canis Minor.

The exception is, he who is born under the sign Virgin, Gemini and the Lynx. From the Lynx, he goes to the *links* of the whole [3] heavenly sheet of signs at the age of seven times

---

[1] Disc becomes dice by syllable cis, (hot) which is water and fire = steam = $ he a M; cis, C I S, see I S, thus C becomes S = sis.

[2] After changing the read, there is still three more ways of reading after the last possible change has been made; so see that there is no *last* change to make in the read, except the *last* one which the reader makes.

[3] The double you hole.

seven, and performs the traditional labors of Hercules — the achievements of Jason, and returns with the Golden Fleece.

The chain which holds all the signs together, is controlled by the power of God, the JEHOVAH of the Bible.

Whale, is whole, as A becomes O by a circle of time. Swallowed by the whale, the whole (all of the) signs of the heavenly arch — the great F *ish* — the I H S of the F from P as ℙ.

From *this*, and *fish*, is the *ish* of the Jew, *His* way of F *ish* in G — fishing.

Cast the net on the O *th* he ℞ (other) side of the ship, and see the haul — hall — all.

Ship, is seen to contain the I H S — *ish* and ℙ. Time and hi ℙ.[1] Net, is ten, ten, is 10 = ①.

Cast the net on the *star* board side while in the flesh, and on the *port* side as the soul bursts through the veil and sees the weather side of existence in the land of Opher — O ph he are — a spiritual existence.

The two fishes of Pisces are connected at the tails by an electrical chain. The first man (Adam) was formed with a thin membraneous connection between the toes and legs, which rotted away like the tail of the polliwog.

The shortest day of the year, the equal day in spring, the longest day in summer, and the equal day in autumn, have all been used, at times, as the last day of the year; and the day following each of those days, has been used as the first day of the first month of the year.

This quarterly division of time in the circle of the year, has been because of the law of the quarterly division in the time of the revolution of the zodiacal belt of signs. That law regulates conception in reproduction of all flesh and blood, cold or warm.

Whatever reason man may make use of, to explain to himself the meaning of his own acts, and the combined results of those acts, and however blind and insensible he may have been or is

---

[1] Thus a ① is a ship; the course of which, is O B the serpent. O B, with the pen added, gives 01 = 10 = ① = B = ① = ① ①. ① ① + ⚇ = Fig. 7 in illustrations.

to this day, or however he may remain so until death, he will *then* wake up as one from sleep, and see all the acts of his life multiplied by 4,[1] which will connect other people's acts with his own : and he will then see that man proposed for God, and that God *dis*posed for man ; he will then cease to worship the images hewn out of the brass of his own imagination.

The names of the astronomical alphabet were given to man directly by Adam, always and forever, and with the law of God.

He was the same man as Thomas surnamed Didymus the twin.   Did, is $\oplus$ and the eye, mus, is the *sum*, and the Y is the crotch, the two ways coupled with one.

The names of letters were the same as those given to things of life, which was because of the likeness· of earthly life to the signs in the heavens.

Two B B s — $\oplus$ $\oplus$ was a bullock.[2]   Two pomegranates was a figure which meant 8.   The letter A displaced to a triangle, was a lamb.   They were offered on the alter ; see how that altering was done : "*done*," is the death of one, the death of Adam. The offering, was "off he are he D."   In *offered*. see off he are D.   Off ered, is deer and reed, re ad D, and read becomes $\oplus$ ear $=$ Bear.

These things are offered to the whole earth on the alter of words ; the changing of the spelling, is the spell in G.   Alter, becomes *alert ;* and in this way language is Castor rated.

Rated, is R ate D.   The way Castor rates words.   Sword is in *words*, by putting time where it can be "taken by the 4 lock" *i.e.*, from right to left — from west to east.[3]   From W to

---

[1] Not meaning the quadruple of his sins or other acts as heaped on himself. The meaning is, that he sees one act of his own, connected with 3 acts of others, and one act of others connected with 3 of his own.   This holds good in the record of his whole life, and is all joined together in rhyme and rhythm.   A man who has been rescued from drowning can tell of his feeling of the outermost edge of that condition which leads on to a spiritual focus.   Rescued, is *re* scued — the time cue of D, skewed on the cross in sheol, where the pin, the skewer, the scue, the scud, the time cud will be eaten at the bidding of the serpent.   The soul then gets its skewer, safety pin, pen, and rib, and is wedded.   Look in wedded, and see *we*, and *bed*, D D $=$ B — $\oplus$.

[2] The "entrails" was the inside meaning of Hebrew.

[3] By death in the darkness of night.

E, est becomes ast — aster see Castor. The alter of the lamb was a fire from heaven — *th* — Z Z.

That portion of the heavens which governs an animal, giving him life and peculiar instincts, had a hieroglyph[1] which was named the same as the animal was named, and so on in all life and sign meaning.

These signs are not mystical in any other sense but that man can get no further than to see that they are so, and that he is gazing directly into the depths of his " well-hole " of knowledge. At this point he is brought to bay — the B (earth) the A (sun) the Y the two ways — the urn and the cup.

The literal killing of animals on a so-called altar, was through ignorance of the 4 meanings of language.

The sign of Gemini is the sign of and for man. When drawn in a simple form it shows man in an attitude of self defence D he fence. Sign in the arms — twins.

Here is self preservation the first law of nature. X is the letter for that sign, the 24th. $2 + 4 = 6$, the sign Virgo — the Virgin. That sign is headless for many reasons; one is, she is the Godhead in the north; another reason is, it means decapitation for the human race, because the soul is pulled from the head by the influence of the sun at the time of death.

Every 2000 years there has been born a child by and under the sign of the Virgin with the link of the twins of May, facing the opposite way from all others of the human race. He was cast cast in the great matrix of nature, and the law exists through that time to the rule that the same thing must take place so long as the earth is in a condition to receive the fulfilment of that law.

Mankind should here see that it is useless to probe these mysteries which are beyond his *see*. He is not in a spiritual condition to grasp the comprehension of Mount Sinai, and the law as there given.

The Mount of Sinai is the cruise which never fails ; souls will see these things on time, and comprehend them as they become

---

[1] Glyph is spiritual.

fitted to the understanding of them. They can *never* do it while in the earthly body.

The spirit is Castor as it leaves heaven, is Mercury on its arrival, and Castor as it enters the neck of the ash body.

The sun child is born of the sign Virgin, with the influence of the planet Venus; the earth receives it secondary, *i.e.*, the influence of the signs which produce the life of the child comes to earth by way of Venus as a connecting link.

He it is who at the age of seven times passed over him, makes a feast and invites his relatives, at the same time he realizes that he is going down the maelstrom [1] of uncertainties. This is in the tale of Belshazzar and Daniel. He is able to read the handwriting on the wall by Castor (Daniel), and then sinks in the ash death of the silent H, the gallows of Haman, and his soul goes into airy space. The body revives and takes a course which is in unison with the course of the soul through sheol, hades, and the home of the damned.

The spirit Castor enters the neck of the dead body, thus regiving the spark of live. This is the miracle of raising the dead. The spirit of Castor, the soul of Pollux, and the earthly body are in unison thrown on to the influence of the sign Ram. The soul in outer space of sheol, and the spirit remaining in the apple core of the neck. So all three are suffering the same things as they compare in harmony. These are the three friends of Job; his wife was his past life — L became W. [2] Job's soul was out of his head. In *boils* is ⊕ soil. He bit the sod — so ◖.
◖ ◗ = ⊕.

From Aries the three pass on to the sign Taurus. They have taken on the strength of Orion, and thus meet the bull. The three stars in line of the sign Orion are in the Hercules belt. That belt is the foundation for naming all things put around the waist.

From the bull the trio pass on to the twins — T wins. In this month the man with his bodily eyes sees his own spirit outside of the body in which it once was, and talks with it. Here

---

[1] Mahal ⚏ row of 12 and M = 13.

[2] Life — wife. L + L = W = V V = X = ⊕.

Saul calls up Samuel by the witch — the double you itch of end ℞.[1] The spirit has enlarged by the gaseous envelope, and has the form of an owl with one eye. It is changing from a soul to a cycloptic spirit.

As all signs are tied together, the trio have to suffer the influence of those which give life to every other kind as well as man.

In the sign Aquari the spirit of Pollux is reduced in size to a spark, and enters the body again, lodging in the same cell it left from at the apex of the optics. Now the spirits Castor and Pollux talk to each other; their voices meet on the palate, and the coat of many colors is given to Joseph.

These are not two ways of thinking as man may suppose. They are spirits: far different from those souls which are in the bodies of all mankind. They do articulate words so to cause a trembling of the flesh of the neck. The purr of the cat is a type — ℙ you are.[2]

The chewing of the cud is another type, and is typical of a spirit doubled in heaven, where all are twins — two in one; of these thou mayest eat by way of Æ ☥ ✕ ☐ ☿.

The deaths and disasters of this epoch of time can be read by the double, and their intensity will be understood to compare with the suffering sun man's experience.

King Herod is the rod of the Virgin, the same as the Angel of the Lord — ah od. That rod is the column of od figures set with the D in Fig. 3. The pun *ish* meant of those who thought fun *ish* meant, was the slaying of the first born. Meaning the reading of deaths (by name) of those who were born for it, by those who discovered the repeat of history.

Man has thought that, if there was a God, he would come directly on to those who sinned, and prove himself; and he could not see but that the innocent suffered while the guilty prospered. The law is astrological; by names, dates, and sums of figures, the suffering circumstances take place.

The soul realizes the personal existent God at the time of death, and sees that it was allowed to make a record for trial.

---

[1] The *ash death*, in which see has, heat, D.

[2] ℙ you are ☐ pure.

In the word incendiary see *diary*. This is a cue to see that
such fire was to take place on time. The D does it. In send I
airy — the D in the air.[1] Destruction by fire and flood — the
huge dell of the deluge. The deluge is death, hell, G and the
law — that huge dell of a 2000 years' whirl of time. The D
(bow) is set in the clouds again for another arc, and the past
time was the flood.[2] As F becomes B by way of the pen and
crook, so flood is blood.[3]

This is the cost of the wreck of time, and the cast of the wreck
of tam. Tam with ◻ (law) is tame ; *tame* is mate = M ate.

The expense of the rib was death and hell in the Styx — the
cruise eye fix on ; no other rout gives the law. Expensive is the
X pen and the sieve — the riddle of Samson. Cost is see host ;
him who was "reckoned without." One word within another
was the scope of his tell († hell) in the tale of Jason searching
for the Golden Fleece ; the tell is cope, his cope.

The conjunction *and* *re* versed is Dan. In eye (high) light
he was cast into L, and suffered the law — the
E ; this gives I E and L to put with Dan, forming Daniel.

The rib of Adam and the *pan* creas is the same
as the spear and left (lee F T) side at the more
modern picture.

Pancreas is Pan, and Ceres goddess of cereals
— the Virgin.

The so-called nails which lay on the ground
at the center cross, have the same meaning as

Fig. 18.

those Egyptian feathers in Fig. 18, *i.e.*, the mend of time
— M end of Tim he — end of time by the ◻.

The crown of thorns shows the suffering in the skull at

---

[1] God, as Jupiter, holds thunder-bolts in his hand, and hurls them on a hair
line ; and he will always strike his own handiwork, if man commits a namable
crime therein. Earthly fire for a lesser crime.

[2] Old time gone, new time come.

[3] The largest cycle of time for the earth is from the changing of the axis to
the same event again, and is the great flood. The smaller cycles and circles are
the same by the law of resemblance. Thus circles of time are all floods by the
law of desolation. At the foot of the 2000 year reign bow is the pot of gold. The
law of the flood can be seen in a yearly circle.

the sculling-place in the letter G, Fig. 2. It is the entire reconstruction of the brain function[1] to suit the incarnation.
The crown of thorns has the same meaning as the older picture of a wreath (writhe) of snakes around the head.

That thorny suffering was always intensified by the looks
and acts of those who believed not, and who would not try to
extend their capacity to the point of understanding.

They cast lots (lost), square ots — cyphers; reckoned him
cyphered out. The coat was without seam — see A M. See
Ham out of the body in pyrthic fire. Same is in seam — Sam E.
The *coat* was the perfect coat of color in the cast of language
given him by his Father. They parted his garments. Gar
meant; the double read. The gar and hole of death is Argo —
the ship of Jason and twins.

------

[1] Fun tye on see T eye on.

CHAPTER XXVII.

EVERY event in the history of this country can be seen to be the work of God in the law by the double read. All of the smallest matters are the same; but man's power of comprehension will fail except on large events.

All of these things are done with the golden threads of the Holy Ghost in three ways, *i.e.* G O and D. This is the power of God and devil.

The names of authors are fitted to the subject they write on, and the names of publishers will all fit the same.

God's work is all done in Hebrew, and when man sees it and can read it, he will know of God this side of the O.

See all disasters by Hebrew. In the word Jefferson see ↲ he double F[1] he are son ☞ son — arson. Van dorn is the front and death horn. Wise is W I see. He who saw double you ↤ him. Double V is † — two right angles same as LL.

In this manner everything has been building since the 10th century, and will tumble down again from the 1st to the 10th in the generation of time to come.

In the word Boston see ☉ ○ ⚵ ○ N; which means the ear *th*, the grave, the cruise, a circle, and N the three — *th* re master.[2]

Boston has the name of "hub"; from hub to hub, is the axle — H. This accounts for names of newspapers there, as well as all other things in the history of that city.

T on is bos; something on T — the brazen serpent ⚵. The double read see half — calf. The leg of Peter is meant, he who sank to Pan the 10th — the goat ✓; he who played for Naiads and Nymphs on the Pandean pipes and the double O boy.

Mack is a name for the sun, and is applied to a man's son. See the merry mac (mc) valley; man you fact you are in G —

---

[1] Double life FF = the hammer.
[2] M aster = 13 the sun star.

manufacturing — the menu F act you ring— ℞ in G. The ring in the ear *th*, in the valley of death; the merry death on the B ridge.

Bos tom,	Boston.
Lo well — low ell,	Lowell.
N *ash* you A,	Nashua.
Man see Esther,	Manchester.
See on cord,	Concord.
N, or *th*, F I hell ◖,	Northfield.
Merry death,	Meredith.
T ill tom,	Tilton.
Sun born tom,	Sanbornton.
New Ham ℘ tom,	New Hampton.
Bell (ble) mount,	Belmont.
All tom,	Alton.
Gill man tom,	Gilmanton.
G ill ford,	Gilford.
Bar N ⚕ head,	Barnstead.
Center Arbor (pole),	Centre Harbor.
Lake O nigh A (laconic),	Laconia.
Bell ≮ nap = pan,	Belknap.
New Ham ℘s higher	New Hampshire.

The *gill* man is he with the jaw-bone. The gill ford was the lock of the jaw in death, where C became G, and D — T.

The name St. Lawrence is he who knew not who he was for seven times seven, and only found it out in death. See that river runs *east*. See fall of ℘ ember ton mill in Lawrence, Mass.

In Manchester read the star man — ester — astar.

In Concord read see on cord (music), hung as Haman, the Ham man in midsummer. See the hanging there of Evans, Pike, La Page and Thomas Samon, and consider their crimes by the names and connections.[1]

---

[1] This allusion to those tragedies is to show the law of forewarnings of things to come, and of echos of things past. Society has to bear such exhibitions of the power of the D, just as long as there is so much pent up wickedness to harmonize with it in the balance of sin. The people of the whole earth may ask themselves how much they have done as individuals toward such outward signs of the work of that same D.

Thomas the sam man, the same man forever. Sam is san and the pen, the *same on* N makes it M. S am the serpent of time and did tempt to the eating — eat in G, the *th* re of Golgotha — *th* re † urn again.

The names of localities in New Hampshire are very pointed at this time. Sunny ℘ lake — Sunapee. Oss I ℘ lake — Centaur double he. Massa be sick — devil's den — D he are — deer — reed — neck — Massabesic. Win I ℘ saw kee — key — ⋉. Win I ℘ see OG — ogee the serpent. Winnipesaukee, the outlet name, and Winnipiscogee, the easterly name. Merry-meeting in Durham. D you are — Ham, death you am.

The names of islands in the great lake, and the accidents, with its general history, can be read with an understanding of astrological law.

See the cutting of Endicut rock — endivet — endicvt end eye see V †. End of time cut and connected again; meaning the bruise of the head and heel of time, the serpent with tail in mouth, the healing of the cycle of time.

The belly of the serpent is the church, bell, and the earth and cup; always right side up.[1] When the soul leaves the body, it sees the brassy fine serpent in the air, and understands the way he goes on his belly, and how cured by the time death, is in the word cursed = ⊂ cures.

Earth is ground, the G round, the G made round as O, where all go through. The soul hears words in the air — the call from God. *Th* is the syllable for the ear; the *th* and ear are earth, and the soul is cast back to earth — to hades.

In this way the cat is let out of a bag of moonshine into the light of the northern heavens. All mankind will have to pass the same course of signs before they can be in the sunlight of understanding.

Their souls will pass along on the path to spirituality, while the bodies, like the caterpillar, will mix with earth and dust.

Change the letters of *sky* to kys, than to syk — ky and see on that alter the name Psyche, the nymph loved by Cupid and made immortal by Jupiter.

---

[1] Back up and backed up.

In both the Bible and the Koran is the law of the connection between earthly and heavenly things, and that connection is the life on earth and the purgatorial path. The same connection is between the build of spelling and pronouncing.

To put a word on the alter (altar) is to make all displacements and all variations of pronouncing, and discover where they all fit in the temple, with their application in the law of God to man.

Ames and hames, mean the midnight sun.[1] Sull means the same. The sull eye van, (Sullivan) means that the low midnight sun will be at the van in the east.

Dogmatical, is God, earth, I see all. The eye of God is on earth, and sees all.

The visible sun is the first eye that a soul has to look to for salvation in the delights of she hall. She, is time he, and the *see* of the H. The work of the Holy Mother is being done at that time.

Another eye will be seen later; so the channel through is by way of the sun. A worship of the sun is not implied, any more than any other part of God's temple. Whatever name religion may be known by, it is all the same rout after death; the utter ℞ out of the wicked, the "utter rout," will be the out utterance of their shameful confessions, their ⚕ utter; you double T he ℞.[2]

In lower-case letters, the p is d, b, q, and they are all dippers by construction; l, is a bolt downward; g, is o and s with a comma, os, so, go, og = ogee.

The c, is a cut circle the same as the capital G, and shows the same law. It is the fifth, as God and the law = Lord. Add c to G, $5 + 7 = 12 = 0$ by 12 months and the circle of the year.

The f, is t with a head on it; meaning the head and cycloptic eye that f gets on the T cross. Thus can all things be matched by observing the law of God in language with cosmography and astronomy.

---

[1] See Amesbury and general history.
[2] ⚕ ⚕ ℞.

By the syllable hor, see that the word *anchor* is the flight of Mercury. The *cat* head is the place for that symbol of hope; see ⚓ and the edge of time, is the kedge. Anchor, is two feet, the cross, and O at the top, the place of a hor sir.[1]

The r, is the head of Pollux dropped over to the right, (*his* left) and his death same as ℞. Any two letters put together in a mix, mean the same deathly cruise.

Hebrew will show itself when one tries to use a dialect with which he is not familiar; he uses it *conversely.* He is apt to shift the pronouns, and will say um, for it, and he, for them and those, and many of the like by change of order. The syllable *um*, is the link which connects languages.

The style of Hebrew is very simple, because it divides all words even to the *letter.* When one finds the place to put those syllables, he can read the language of God to man.

Will the children of eye is real look [2] at the words *pate*, and ball D.[3] See illegitimate; sick he get a mate; re born double without earthly parents. Legitimate, is leg it eye mate, or lee G it him ate,[4] etc.; Dan so 4 *th* for ever.

Synonym. Sin on Y eye M. The soul in sin on Y, goes to M — the sun as an F in the air. See it suffers equatorially; so *fair*, is equitable and just. By the J you st, is *just.*

A *guard*, is secure. G you hard, see cure. When the soul with sin gets on M (13) in sheol, sin is on M, sinonm — synonym. As all words fit the outer court of the temple, so can synonyms be understood.

Ration, is a ray, and the soul on T, eating; see ration, is *grub;* that soul gets into G, and cast to hades as a grub — the G rub. Rub is is *bur* — the pricks of that eye none can kick against.

This is the way to account for the blending of synonyms.

This man, so often mentioned in this book, can be found by letting down the bar on T, putting the H directly over it, with

---

[1] Hawser.   [2] Israel.   [3] Bald.

[4] Lees, are dregs. In *eldest*, is lee, eel, led he ⚵ ; by doubling the letters and using the reed, the meaning of the eldest son can be reached = ℞ each he ⊂ = re ache ⊃.

the I to the left and the S on the right. See *this* the superscription.

Divide " this " in half and see *th* and *is* — fire from heaven is. So does all language run — up to the eye of God, down to hal below, or still lower down to hel, to hol. See the many ways of punning the word holocaust. The holy cause †.

If man says it is against reason and common sense to consider those things as the work of God, he should see the D and shaft of od numbers. It is O D So the flood goes on, the F, two circles and death. All there is for man this side of the vale is hope in faith.

Man will say the " big fish eat the little ones," without thinking of himself as a smelt = smell T, so soon to be swallowed by the T rout (trout) which all must travel to know these things.

A smile, the same as music, is one of the connecting links between earth and heaven ; so he who does not smile, for the sake of sanctimony, is like him who will not attend at a theatre because he thinks it is the work of the devil ; while in his heart he will have to admit that the fine sentiment there expressed, the music, scenery, and the lesson to be learned by the triumph at the *last* of the good and true, all taken together, *do* touch him in a very tender spot. That spot is his *soul* which is longing for spiritual bliss.

The same is true of worship in God's holy temple. There is a desire for a continuance of life beyond the grave, and more knowledge. It is the same soul feeling darkly for that light of immortality which is inspired by the truth of its progressive condition.

People of this age think the Romans of 2000 years ago were very wicked. So *very* wicked, that, although they saw him raise the dead,[1] convert water into wine, and produce bread for thousands to feed on, they were hardened in heart, and sought

---

[1] The tales in the gospel of bringing the dead to life and healing the blind, deaf, and the sick generally, apply *first* to the sun man ; but because of the signs in the heavens which brought it about, many people were affected the same way, and were found to be alive after being pronounced dead. The same of diseases. It will be seen in names and localities as by the Hebrew read — reed — *re* D, *re* ed hed, *re* head — life.

to destroy him who they could but know was not to be blamed for anything.

Had he done those things on a low base of language,[1] would they have shunned or mobbed him? The same natural laws existed then as at this time, and the tales in the Testament are true by the double read — the G O spell — the law of seven and one — the temple.

People have a great wonder why men so low could be found as to lay hands on Him. Has it ever dawned on the minds of this enlightened people, how a man would be received who should betray that Master again, and in their day.

That Master was the spirit of the Archangel, and was betrayed by the body in which it was, by the ⋉ is S. So they sought to lay hands on him.[2]

His looks and appearance did not agree with their ideas of Hercules with the ponderous club, or of Apollo in divination; and they knew him from birth, and saw him not in death. His masterly utterance, and his condemnation of sin and wickedness, they would not listen to.

"Behold this man eateth with sinners." This is a text for many a sermon, and people are moved to tears by it. They worship the record of his lowliness, which always was and will be forever.

They look for him in power and great glory. ℘ oh double you he ℞ is power, and G square or and the urn is glory. Or is gold from the land of O ℘ H he ℞ — Opher. Hebrew the Bible, and Jew like, understand the double read of straw bricks.

How would a soul cast into hades feel to be received as one who had always been there, and never to leave, — to always remain an imp in that abode, and tortured by demons, because it

---

[1] Earthly strictly.

[2] They said he was not to be blamed for anything which he did or said, for he did not know what he was doing. They led him to a place which added to his suffering, and he as Peter had to say I " knew him not," in order to obtain his liberty. Peter was forgiven and pardoned from on high, but the wrath of God came on to that people. He called on God to forgive them. In *forgive* is forge, the eye and V. With this language God does his work on earth and in heaven. Pardoned is ℘ hard one D, ℘℞◖ on D.

said it came out of a body on the earth? These things put as questions, are no idle comparison.

He did betray himself as in a story by his name J you sad — J you D *as* — he died *as* ☽, which is the astrological meaning of Judas. J for June[1] and das for sad.

These heavenly truths are earthly riddles, but not the *less* true.

Of course, he would betray himself for all reasons which may appear. Not the least of which reason is the fact that he was an honest man and did eschew evil[2] = Levi. He ate that part of the tree in Pisces — the house of Levi. Eschew is he time chew, and became a Jew, as all will be in heaven. Look at the Almanack man to see a picture of the same suffering Judas. There is the man and the manual, Immanuel in the womb of nature by the sun instead of the moon, also the moon and sun.

God does not shape the law and salvation scheme to fit the ideas of moonlit children, or place it in tales which would not fit anywhere, except on earth. The law is such as to pick men out of bondage and ignorance.

The Romans of 2000 years ago were kind and sympathizing as people of to-day are, and would not have knowingly done as they did. It was because they were frozen in ignorance the same as people of this age.[3]

Worship the Bible as it reads, with an understanding that man is saved from his ignorance, and not for his much knowledge; for his knowledge is his ignorance. In its mysteries he should discover that there are blessings beyond this earth.

There is but one theme in the Bible for man. He should follow that theme, and wait for time to see how the variations cover that theme.

Man has built up theories on the variations of that theme, un-

---

[1] ☽J you knee.   [2] He was a spirit with *truth* — true *th.*

[3] Man does not realize how short a time 2000 years has been, or that nature was just the same then as now. It is all the same as yesterday. Man measures time by the seeming length of his own life, and judges of God's work by the same. Man should search deep into his own knowledge to discover the reason for the unbelief of the Romans, and should see that the proofs of an advent are always the same. If he cannot *see* it, he should reason the same in *it*, as in all other things. The law of God is not out of reason, being perfect, the same as the temple.

til the simple air has been lost. The air is the song; place " song " upon the alter — altar.

Man is but half, and does never see but one fourth at a time. This is his make up, but he does know better than to be cruel, for he does not like to be tortured, and he does realize that he knows not from whence he came or whither he is going.

The three Ts and the Xs in the cruise through purgatory will show the soul the way to spiritual music in thought and expression, and why language is Hebrewed to reach the everlasting law of God. He brews that way — *th* at way. A T — the 20th century.

Fire is F ire, F higher. Ire is temper. Re is the doubling on the cross, the being born again ; so *re*, with the eye, is *ire*. This takes place in the H, so ire is hire — high he R — higher.

Earthly fire changes fibre to gas. Put fibre and gas on the alter, and see the law of destruction and re construction.

In tion and sion see shun. Shun is time, temple U (H G) and N the leave $= 14 = 4$ T en $= \oplus$.

The book of Ezekiel is the law of an advent and its consequences. In the name see he Z he kill.

The book opens with the thirtieth year, fourth month $= 3 + 4 = 7 = G$, and a cypher $= 15 = $ God. The fifth day $= $ the letter $\mp = $ weasel $= $ we, A and S century and el $= $ hell.

See he bar, bear, she bear. He was the son of Buz eye $= \oplus$ you Z high, and was slain as Isaac.

In the second chapter of that book see Castor enters the body of Pollux, and gives the law ; a book " written within and without " (two ways). In the third chapter he eats the roll, the two sided his cuit (see cute) see you *it* $= \mp$, eats R oh LL.

He found (by the eating of the fruit) the same honey in the carcass of the Lion.

CHAPTER XXVI.

Man should read the Bible for many reasons, however he may fail to understand some parts of it. There is enough to show the power and love of God.

From Judas,[1] to Judas Iscariot; Juda with his chariot, Nimrod, Jehu, Apollo with the same chariot which Phæton drove and was hurled into Eridanus — death and hell. Char, is smouldering fire; eye ot is death; the whole is chariot. The two wheeled vehicle takes its name from Fig. 7.

Red hair, is called spica. It is because of the same heavenly fire, and that bright star in the ear of corn (C horn) in the sign of the Virgin — Virgo; from which is vital, vitality, and virtue, and virtually is salvation by the same fiery course. All will be reborn of God — the G, O and D, G I D O and G.

Consider the depopulation of the Nile, and the destruction of Babylon and Nineveh, and study well those names. It was so in the valley of the Ganges, and the Hoang Ho.

See the names of destructive things that have their foundation in the sign Gemini, and the A S century, and profit by the lesson to be learned in the reading of history.

As (in the law) F becomes B, read, F he B, ℞ you airy.[2] U is hairy. The circle of life connects in the air from Pisces to Aries. If it fails to connect, Aries becomes Arez. Z in place of *is*. From arez, is araze, raze razee. Z meaning destruction at the "Tekel" place. In Arez is Ezra. Arez, is lightning and era.

At this jumping off place, is the *joint* — join T, the hairy joint — the joint neir. Fury and bury are in February, also ebreu and fare — the grub — menu.[3] Grub, is *bury* — a hole — H lo Ƹ, ☐.

---

[1] Pollox, ☉ you ☽ as, S ad for Judas.   [2] February.

[3] Grub, is also called fodder = F od ☽ he are. Here is again seen the law that the soul as F must eat of the fruit until the ☽ is reached, where it doubles as W the 23d letter; 2 + 3 = 5, the weasel and law ☽ = I = ☽ I D=☉.

The scales of the fishes of February are the balance in which the soul is caught and wayed — double you *aye* D.

When the moon is turned to blood,[1] it does not give the 1st day of Aries; the sun gives the day, and it is the *last* day, the 30th of Pisces,[2] so called because the soul is thrown out of the circle of its former adjustment, and gone to eat of the pass over (Passover) of the Styx.

That 30th day is the lap on from the moon's influence on to the sun's time and influence. There and then it betrays itself for 30 Pisces (pieces) of silver, and starts on the cruise I fix on. In silver is siiver — time and liver — live ℞.

That 30 days, is 30 Pisces off sliver. The 30th day of Pisces, would be the *last* day — the first day of Arez. This is for leap years. 29 Pisces fit 3 years out of 4. He betrayed himself in leap year at the heel — heal of time.

The heal of time by the eater piece, is in everything in nature this side of heaven. See it in music between B and C, when the A is at concert pitch; the B natural has to be played a little sharp when doubled with G, and it is the key of H, the same silent mystery.

As the one day added for leap year, and the cancelling of a day periodically, does not quite account for the regulation of time, there is a wise provision made for it from heaven.

The length of time which the sufferer lay dead during that year, is just the amount of time that is cast out, *i.e.*, the distance is shortened on the orbit.[3] This is the finest of the adjustment, and is the heavenly leap year when the woe man pays the penalty.[4]

---

[1] The moon is red, and the color of blood, at the time of the earth's quarter turn on its axis. H eat (heat) ye all of *it*.

[2] The leper's day is the 29th, 3 years out of 4.

[3] Orbit, obit; oh bit by God; the *real* hydrophobia. High dry 4 by A. That which set the jaw against ☾ ℞ in ♓. See the *real* mumps. That bite was the bight, ☉ hight, the loop, the road, the stretch of orbit taken up to true time on the earth's course. This is the foundation of all diseases on earth, as can be seen by names and diagnosis. Die a G know S *is*, the serpent. Die a G nose is — cat ℞. M you see us — mucus — us cum — come — scum — the cream of the milky word — the mill key.

[4] The womb man paid the bills.

See that everything is material, and that God cares for it all, including man and his ignorance. He also provides for his wickedness by a punishment which he cannot escape. God is alike in time, mercy, and vengeance. The whole is justice.

The " potter's field " is the P and the ots — the cyphers of his deaths. Judas was hanged as Haman, and his bowels gushed out — he out of balance — suffered Liber. Gush is G hush = the hush of death as in Fig. 2, the game of seven up.

Eli is the law and lye. Lye is L ye; from the urn of death to the eye — Y to eye — he L eye — Eli.

There are four stories in unison in the gospel; Three are Peter, Thomas, and Judas. They all unite to make the fourth, the same as three seasons of the Jews are four and the year.[1]

In Peter, see that P is T, and T is R, and that *pet* is R. In Judas see Juda and the serpent — T he M P O, tempo.

If this man used the pronoun I as applying it to any incident of his past life, it would not fit, because the I that once was, was no longer the same I. His death and entire reconstruction displaced the former I. His first I (Belshazzar) was not the I of any part of the two years' suffering;[2] neither was his last I. From the Eli is lie. He could not say that which would be the truth to man, if he said I, as applied to the business of the past.

For this reason was the story of Ananias and Sapphira written. He lied unto God. In his case a lie to man, was Eli to God — he lie G to God. Thus, man's knowledge of the foundation gave the power to write so many different tales of some portion of the cruise I fix on. Man knows not what he says by the law of 4.

The rib is the club of Hercules with which he slays all monsters in the pathway of light,

Bread from heaven is the reed of B. Bread is O *re* ad; the d to add to ad was F = Deaf; the deafness of that adder was death. See why a snake is an adder and called a serpent.

In the word flood find fool and death. See a fool in Taurus, and that a parable is a pair in the sign of the bull, the full yoke of mythology — the double read.

---

[1] Same as the fiery furnace.

[2] And yet it was, but at last he was first.

The syllables all, al, ol, el, il, etc., all carry to the she hall = sheol.   Ory, ry, ly and those which end with Y, carry to the urn ; from which comes life by A.   Omega becomes Alpha Y △ A.

"Moses stretched out his hand, and the east wind parted the sea" = see C.   Hand was the temple and the C on junction[1] = conjunction *and*, re versed is Dan — the connection of heavenly language with earthly words ; the east wind was ꓷ , where his circle of life was cut at Pisces.[2]

Forty years in the wilderness ; the law of 4 and the O.   In this way the children of Israel walk and they get the man A (manna), the bread.

In Moses see 13, the O and time doubled.   In Aaron, hair on, air on, air oh N = 14.

Everything is correctly named for the epoch of time as it passes along.   Mankind are adjusted to these things unconsciously, because it is the perfect law of God set in the heavens.

All "slang phrases" are the result of the phase of the signs of the heavens above, in the earth beneath, and the waters beneath the earth.

People of to-day are walking the earth and wondering about the unfathomable, without ever thinking of looking up to the keys — kys — sky, the Y ks — why keys of heaven.   Who stops to think of what is meant by "*the heavens,*" so often mentioned in the Bible.   There is declared the glory of God, and man can look and worship with rejoicing.   Mankind have come to the worship of the image of God as drawn in their own imagination, the same as the Egyptians did when swamped in the red see of the sea = C.

The reason why people have not believed in the law when given, was for the same reason that the people of to-day do not look for this explanation of those stupendous mysteries, the attempt to solve which has caused wars and untold sufferings, with the downfall of empire after empire.   They are looking for

---

[1] Air junction. See history of Ayer Junction, Mass. The Grow tom = Groton = G rot on.

[2] See fire at Eastport, Maine.

things to take place here, which they are to see out of the body and in other spheres. It is in man's nature to expect those things because he is immortal.[1]

This will all be known to be the correct interpretation of the law in time, by pun is meant the double read of events; the developing of the mysteries in the silent H.

The present is a time of God's work in showing up the wickedness and sin of the earth by murder, defalcation, forgery, and fraud; the names of those engaged in it will be found to agree with fires, shipwrecks, and disasters of all kinds. The whole are on the present epoch of time by names, dates, and sums of figures.

In disaster, see D is a star; that star is Procyon $=$ P roe see Y on. With the crook it becomes *broken* by pronunciation. Murder is 13 $=$ 4 you are death he are. Date is death ate. Star is $ a R.

The present condition of the earth is that darkness that can be felt. All feel a want of light thrown on to the subject here presented, because of the great diversity of opinion among men.

If man try to read deep into language, *i.e.*, beyond two meanings, he gets into never-ending disputes; for it is all his experience beyond this earth where it will come easy, and be all easily understood. It applies three there and one here, four in all.

Look at the boasted enlightenment of the 19th century in a free (?) country. See a bill introduced to relieve *sane* persons now confined in public and private asylums in the District of Columbia.

See the names in the combined machinery of government, and consider the bolt of lightning on the Capitol the 21st of Aries '88, and the fire in the basement — base is meant.

The forget of the fagot, is man's weakness. The fagot and

---

[1] The A and S century is the tail of time, and always brings with it many strange and unreasonable beliefs, called isms $=$ miss. The T ake (ache) added, gives mistake with a single S. These are the "strange wives" in the book of Ezra. In the law of resemblance there has to be a large percentage of marraiges which prove unpleasant, the same as the strange and unhappy ideas which man has of God at this time. *Creed* is the C reed, see read — the O pen in G (opening) in the R he $\complement$ $=$ red, see A $=$ sea.

the eye, is the fagoti, — the double reed (bassoon) pipe. The fire of that pipe is the toe backer from the north. See Fig. 7.

Man has become so accustomed[1] to destruction, that he has but little remembrance of it, except[2] as he suffers himself.

Put match on the alter; one leg[3] is T Ham, if you see C.

The amusing way of the muse is M you see, the A muse in G, M sue in G.

The naming of heavenly signs by man has been connected with some earthly history; that history has had some connection by similarity with the suffering and trials of him who was kept alive in body, while the soul was struggling in the perils of sheol and hades.

That history seems exaggerated, because it fits both the earth and the heavens together, by a scale of comparison of which man knows but little. These are the trials and triumph of soul and body together, and must read as exaggerated in order to be put into letters.

Because man makes use of these same letters on a lower base of land gage, he cannot see reason in the way mythology has to read, *i.e.*, the letter arrangement.

Mythology reads for heaven, earth, and hell. Earthly comparisons seem used, because man knows of nothing further along. Those tales must have the stamp of mystery, or man would explain them all away, and sink in darkness and ignorance of even worldly matters.

The eternal fitness of language *is* so, not because man has so placed it by his studies in the scale of progression alone, but because it is so written in the heavens, and it comes to man a free gift,[4] the same as the law of music.

Man takes the credit for what he does, and wonders why it was never done before. Man can do nothing which does not fit the time in which he lives, and that part of the serpentine path on which the firmament is moving.

---

[1] Accost tom, he died. A see cost.

[2] X see he P T — the twin.

[3] One of four ways.

[4] See the "dead give away" of a dead gift — ꟻ †.

Fig. 19, is an illustration of vibration of the heart. It is the same as between G and A, and the death place is between the long and short points. The jump by and over that place is made at every beat, and is the same law as the closing by the moon's circle from heel to head.

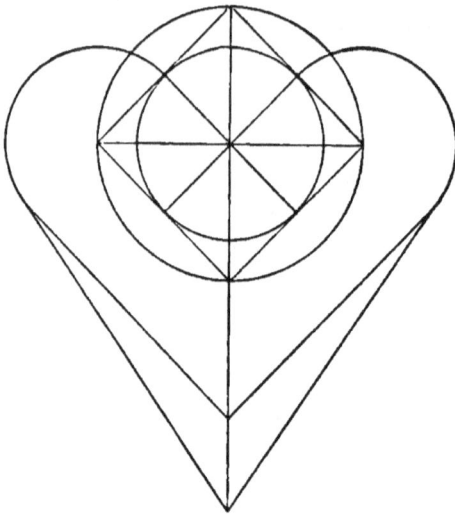

Fig. 19.

If one of anything be cut in two, and one part cast away, and the remaining part cut in two and so on, there never would be an end to the work so long as the *last* piece could be found. The "*last* piece," is the eater piece to be devoured.

Apply this law to the finest adjustment of the length of the earth's orbit by all divisions given, and see the human race carried over by the death of one man.

Thus are Julian periods accounted for. Juli, a N the lion from lye on, the ash death.

The animal which bears that name is a type of the sun man by the mane; *re* verse, is name. That mane is the H air of Mary[1] which surrounds the head and neck, and is invisible to children of the moon's time.

Every animal and vegetable known to man are types of this same re double work, and the name and habit will fit the case. It can be found easy by English at this epoch of time, because the fruit was eaten in that dialect last.

Ɛ becomes I, by the four-sided square with a dot, and it is the sign of the weasel.[2] Here is the double you easel of the painter, and the right angles of the cross.

See the word *you.* Y is the three sticks of A, where the *last*

---

[1] M = 13 = 4 in the air.

[2] See frontispiece — law of desolation.

becomes first, and O is the hole of holiness.[1] U is the silent magnet in the air and earth : that which controls all life and inanimation.

From earn, to urn ; the sweat, of the F ace. In *sweat*, is A and west ; a cross line of his adjustment to the pole line. *So*, Adam earned his bread — ear N H is ☉ read = dear.

Sweat is ℙ her spire, S pire pyre — time fire.

The sign Capricornus (Pan), is the letter V with a circle on it, which means that the V is united with and changeable to B as $v = v$. That sign also means the Virgin with the boy in her arms. See Saint Thomas' day — Christmas. The syllable *tom*, is seen to be the cross, the grave and M = 13 the sun's number in the law.

By analyzing the word ascension, it will be seen that it is another account, and another way of telling the story of N at the A and S of time. Sion, is time and eye (9) on, and includes the rout of the Pyrrhic traveller.

While yet he was talking, he was taken you ℙ (up) out of sight ; yet he was seen by many afterward, *i.e.*, the body was known to be the same as had been seen. The four ways of heavenly reading disjoints all of man's efforts to write the story.

---

[1] Hole he see, hole Y C, H ole see, the hole *he* see was O ; see holy see. The *diet*, was time, (S) urn, (Y) ; N, (△) O, (15) death (☾) the whole was synod, — the congregation of all the signs, — the whale. Diet, is *tied* — from 6 + 6 to 7 + 7. 6 + 6 = 12, 7 + 7 = 14 ; 12 + 14 = 26, the Z from Alpha to Omega. He leaned = lean he died on the name John, as J on H the beloved = ☉ loved = love ☾ ; as V becomes B by $v = v$, so *love*, is square O B E the serpent. No one dialect includes the law.

CHAPTER XXVII.

The death and transfiguration of Hercules has been shown in many ways in the statuary and bas-relief of past ages. The Assyrians showed it by the representation of a man pinned to the ground, and his skin being stripped off by man.[1] Those pictures gave rise to the idea that those people did skin their war captives. So people of 4000 years hence may think that men of this age did tie and nail their captives to a cross and the letter T.

The condition of a soul in the body of a man is the same as malt; and purgatory is the same as the distillery;[2] see the fitness of all names in connection.

A soul being malt, it is an undeveloped spirit held captive in the flesh. It places all things on a belief, and honestly believes that upon that belief rests the surety of its soul salvation.[3] It thinks God is angry with those who have not the "*right* belief."

This is all, because the spirit is undeveloped. People cling tenaciously to their preconceived ideas because of the moon's influence. They become irritable if they meet any opposition, because born under different aspects. They wish to keep on worshipping the images of their own imagination. This is all in nature. About 30 days of progress by the moon's circle, and that is the extent; the body is then put on to another thirty days, and so on. In that way the mind of man is held with the body, and he feels the limit of his understanding. His power of ready comprehension fails, and he takes to the slow process of study. Here he slowly adds idea after idea, without thinking of the perfect connection of those ideas by language and circumstance.

---

[1] See why man believes in but one advent.
[2] By the law of typical representation.
[3] It knows not the sole — 30 silver piece rout.

God himself exists independent of the herein-described mathematical law. His number being 15, is the connection with man, and man's connection with and in the law — ⊙.[1]

The letter D, and those od numbers set to that letter in Fig. 3, is the devil. It is the column (call em) by which he leads men around, tempting them to do all sinful things. In this way God has fought all wars, and brought misery on to earth as a punishment for man's refusal to accept the law.

Two LL s twice make an H. The lap is 4 double on the perch — the trap of the H gallows. Four L s make an ∟, so ∟ becomes ⊢ — the □ ▢ ⊠ ▢ the weasel hole through[2] the law.

The ferret is the two crooks on a staff, the stalk, S talk, and is the unity and the fineness of the infinite ÷ in fin eight.

Od is made even by adding the *last* D, as in odd. The D leads man into all manner of sin and wickedness, and causes him to commit all namable crimes. It requires man's nature with it, in order to succeed as the D. This is the natural way to handle man, because of his od construction.

Man is always trying to get even, but in trying for even, he gets od; which is his all that side of the sun's path.

Soul, sole the cobler's last — the 12 foot — the *last* day; that day the moon will not transfer the thread = *th* read of life from Pisces to Aries; *i.e.*, make the life jump from the foot to the crown of the head.[3] Then is the moon turned to blood, and the soul goes marching on another experience.[4] Then take place many of those things which men have honestly believed would take place on earth at the *last* day,[5] as they, in their mind, saw it.

The commanding the sun to stand still, applies to a time when the earth will take a turn at the shifting of its axis. That event will take place again and again for ever. It is the way, it is heated up from time to time, so to retain astronomical life.

The principle of the musical octave being the law throughout the great universe, no one of the planets can be thrown out of

---

[1] The hole of the grave.   [2] *th* rough.
[3] Also the day the axis is shifted.   [4] See Fig. 4.
[5] There is a *last* day for each and all.

place or destroyed without changing the law of harmony as it exists everywhere.

When the earth is cold it shakes like ague. In *ague* is age and the magnet. Ague leads to fever and heat, and the changing of the axis.

The meaning of the astronomical alphabet was kept within a set who thought themselves fitted by a sort of royal imagination to give the law without showing the foundation. For this sin God showered od numbers on to earth, and overturned empires and cast down thrones.

The white race are now again the Jews, and have a chance to make their history for the next 2000 years. The reason why the Jews were loth to accept the sun man was, because they saw nothing but the workings of nature, and they made in their minds a separation between nature and God. They could not see that God used the forces of nature, and they realized not the fact of there being things in nature of which they knew nothing, because of the coarseness of their senses. If with their eyes they could have seen the air, they would have had no doubts.

℞ read Jew dice. ℞ red you die see. ℞ red you ◖ ice cold pole. See prejudice.

Theories are known by names. People gradually become prejudiced against a theory and its name. The cause of such phenomena was once well known, and it was recognized by counting goddess Diana among the heads of written law.

It is the ever one face of the moon and its four weeks' work on man, the phase and phiz. Thus, a person who can listen to a preacher with interest, while he talks of purification and the route to heaven after death, may be shocked beyond his own explanation, if the word *purgatory* is used.

See in potatoes the top and pot, ate and toes of Pisces. They are tubers, the base of music — 2 bears.[1] Two B he are, see Fig. 7. Bug is ⊕ hug — the hug of the she-bear. Slug is time and the square hug. In root is O and rot; from this rot is the tree of life.

---

[1] The spelling is the rough; the speaking, the blending.

The difference between root and rot is as two lives from one. The doubling of a letter is its recurrence in the life to come.

The place from which the eatables and syllables come, is the alphabetical tree where Adam ate. The serpent did tempt (time) him in the night and darkness of his ignorance — the Eve in G, evening. He himself was the womb man — woman.

See the learning of the author of that story, and understand that person was a Christian and Pagan.

Twenty-five letters represent that number of signs in the heavens that Adam had to suffer under during his fall and death unto a new life on earth. He suffered on earth what others suffer after death.

Although the word suffer is used, there is much pleasure mixed with it, and that fact is, why the law seems to be written in a serio comic way.[1]

Letters[2] are astronomical and astrological, because, as the eye of God looks over the heavens, the orbits as they cross each other are seen to form these same letters. When two orbits cross each other at a short distance apart, a fiery letter is formed which retains its appearance much longer than when and where the distance is great; and the crossing of that point by another planet will regulate the intensity of that letter.

Draw three lines across a sheet of paper in three directions, and find A at the triangle. In like manner all are formed.

This earth is ruled by twenty of those letters, which by sounds[3] are compressed to sixteen or extended to twenty six. Those letters are "fiery" because of the antagonism of their electrical traits. Thus is the history of the earth written with a pen of fire at the time of the fulfilment.

In the Pyrrhic dance,[4] is to be seen the cruise. There is the

---

[1] Man knows that he is himself guilty of changing the Bible in his mind, so to avoid hell and punishment. He expects that the chosen leader of the race has suffered for him. When he has to bear the consequences of his own sin, he will know that the sun man did have to do the same thing.

[2] Letters, are square setters, also *re* $\ddagger$ tell = † hell. Shell, is sh he L L = † the place where the kernel is stripped from the cob — see O B.

[3] By the sound of words the bottom is reached; this is why shoal (show all) water is a sound.

[4] Chambers' Ency., vol. 8.

Virgin enthroned on the dome — the inverted bowl. See bit of frieze with 5 balls on top, and 7 dots twice on the face of it.

The circular figure of which there are 4, is the circle of life, the cross and 4 holes, the same Thomas put his finger into, and the principle of the Maltese cross.

Two have no holes; they are not yet made by the sufferer. One is oblong — O B L on G.

Pyrrhic dance.

The body of the sufferer is the lower center figure. His soul is pulled out, and the left hand of that soul rests upon the head of the body it left. Those feet presented to the Virgin, mean Pisces. On the toes of one foot is the vase (Y) with two sprigs, (the double nature) and on the other toes (the right) is the bone — the rib of Adam, the pen; underneath is the urn, the death, — ashes.

Urn, is you are N = 14, 1 + 4 = 5 — the law; see 5 dots

on the cap of that soul, and there is the fiery tassel on the cap. The column, is the shaft of od numbers set to the ⊄ which he dies on and under.

The figure at the lower left, is the persecutor of the body; his spear is broken and he has become harmless.

The figure at the lower right is the hind — the guardian angel with the flaming sword who protects that exposed body for that time. She has the mantle for Elisha, and the coat of armor.

The long sided square with the ramp on it, represents the amount of time he was born to live, and the cause of his death. It is composed of 13 lines; the outside 4 lines which make the field, mean death. He turned 3 weak corners, and met death at the 4 *th*.

The inside grating[1] is 9 lines — the ⊀at;[2] 4 outside lines for the 2d circle of life, and 5 bars — the law and Lord's number. The can,[3] has a band around it, inside of which is placed the ancient tuning fork or lyre — meaning music which gives him Apollo. On the cover, is the serpent of time = the worm. It is the ⊀, — the cork-screw which opens the can of mysteries. The calker drives oakum (O come) into seams, and saves the hull, and the whole, at the hole of time.

The 4 diamond shaped figures, on 3 of which is the cross, are to represent the rhombus. The 4th one between the legs has only a dot as yet, for he has not died the first death. The whole scene is the experience in the month Pisces, the sinking into lye ashes and water, — the commencement of the laborous tasks of Hercules, — the cruise to India and return.

The rhombus is represented 4 times so to give 8000 years, the temple of time.

See a B, see another B the 2 ① ① of Fig. 7. See a B cab. This is why a cab has its name — 2 wheels and one door, Herdic, all the same from Herald.

From this *cab*, is see abl, cable and cabal. See a ball, see a bull, cabalistic, and cabalism of the Jews has its origin at that two ball eye and cross in the northern heavens. They are Ursa Major and Minor. The eye is the pole of the heavens.

---

[1] Great in G. [2] Cat, chat, see hat.
[3] Cancer, can ser, can sir.

CHAPTER XXVIII.

The Griffin, the unicorn, the sea-serpent, the mermaid, the lion with a man's head and a coat of mail around the neck terminating in wings behind the head, all mean the same Pyrrhic traveller — Callisto.[1]

All animals, reptiles, birds, insects, fishes, and all life whether cold or warm blooded, have a restorer reborn to them at periodical times the same as man. This is a repetition of the law of forces that acted at the first creation of the same life; were it not for this fact, that life would dwindle down to the obsolete in a few centuries, and become extinct.

See B B s and ants.[2] There is the place for hard sluggers to go to learn a thing 0 2 — ought to[3] learn the double reed; ant, nat, tan = T is N. Sluggard was he who would not try to read the signs of the times.

The heavenly sheet of signs and their arrangement always govern articulation, and cause all slang phrases; phases do it.

As time goes on, the eternal rounds of language change gradually and very softly, so the meaning of many words seem to undergo a change. This is self adjusting, unknown to man, and unrealized in his short history.

Hebrew is always the same astrological law, and easy to read by letter sign application.

In some of the older parts of the Bible, there are words and syllables of which the present race have not a clear understanding. This is because of the changing of the aspect[4] of the heavens. Those fiery letters are continually burning the law of the present edge[5] of time, the ax and acts.

---

[1] See C all is toe to two, his toe.

[2] Ant S ante on time; ℘ is M higher, M ire, M I are he = pismire.

[3] Hot two, hot to.

[4] P he see T at the A and S of time is the present aspect.

[5] Edge with C ☐ is colledge; he of the D knows the college, see all he G he.

This is the law of language, and has never been changed, not one jot or one tittle.

From cubes with balls in them, to balls with cubes in them, shifting[1] back and fourth (4th) continually, is the geometrical way of expressing the vibrations in nature ; this is a "far fetched" comparison, and is absolute.

From one to the other, all through space is this thing going on, and is universal life, the beatings of the heart of nature.

Earthly mathematicians may work fractions, and think that they are squaring the circle of their lives here, and by good conduct[2] will be accepted direct to heaven with all of their hoarded earthly knowledge ; but in purgatory they will become an infant, and cry to the Holy Mother for mercy.

Plunged into sheol with all their earthly knowledge, they must lay it all aside, and become as the least, in order to know the kingdom of even. O is the even letter, and through that, on the other side of the curtain,[3] is where and when things even up.

Man here[4] has hope in faith for a line to follow, but he who has tortured his kind must be forgiven ere he can pass on with that hope line. There is a punishment swift and sure for all of man's misdeeds.

All disputes about theology are never-ending, and a source of sorrow in sheol.[5] Hope on, hope ever, with prayer and penitence. The lowly here will not have to be lowered in the course of purgatory, that course where all are brought to a level — eve LL.

The soul entering the cruise of purgatory, hears its name called by the voice of God, and he is thus guided along to spiritual life ; so he need not think to know the way while here. He can be kind and honest here, and all those things in th all ogee (theology) which are to be needed, will be added to him on

---

[1] Sh I F T in G.   [2] See on D you see † , conduct.

[3] Curtain is sertain — certain, etc.   [4] On earth.

[5] When man tries to establish a belief in a hell, he naturally thinks of children, and his nature revolts; he forgets that God is allwise, and knows man by root and branch even to the leaflet. Children are all saved from any such consignment as some men have accused other men of believing in. None feel any punishment but that which is exacted by a heavenly court of justice. Children are not to be punished for that they know not of. Mankind are the work of God, and are in his hands, and *his* ways are just and kind.

time, and by God directly, and with a never failing surety. It is a very simple thing to inherit immortality, so far as a knowledge of earthly matters is concerned, or so far as a foreknowledge of heaven goes; for *no* one has any conception of its realities, and to attempt to blindly lead the blind is an error. All are in the same mode of conveyance, from those who think they are high, to those who are willing to be low. Low counts one the same as high, and 4 = the letter D is the game.

On ⊙ on — onion. The Egyptians are said to have worshipped the onion. See the doubled life of the onion, parsnip, turnip, beet, etc., and put those names on the altar, where the typical nature will be discovered.

Those people recognized the arrow MA[1] (aroma) in the air, and knew of an unseen power in their midst; it was the hawk eye — nine.

They were loth to believe in Jonah as the messenger, and could not think of a spirit as being matter. They were the same as people of this epoch who cannot think of anything but the body, because their own soul has not yet been required.

They thought of his body only, and thought he spoke of his body as they did of their own.[2] They knew not of the midnight deaths.

As no man saw the creation or recreation of the first man, so no man has ever seen those deaths or the recoming to life. Man is willing to believe these things, if he sees them, but God has forbid that he ever shall see them.

Could a man's imagination lead him to think that these things had taken place with him, if they had not? and could all these things take place with a man, and he not know all about it? and could this law exist and not be applicable in nature and with a

---

[1] Aroma is Roma — a roamer — one who roams in sunlight. Row M he ℞. The roam through sheol where the $ in K (stink) is. Purification in heavenly fire; that square ache of brimstone. The work of nature in transforming a soul into a spirit.

[2] They knew he claimed to speak of the spirit, but they thought he was mistaken in himself. They claimed to know him better than he knew himself, after all of his experience. That experience they would not admit, because they had it not themselves. See ruins of mighty empires as the result.

man? If not, then man must admit the fact of one being born for it, and his having to meet it all on time.

Of course, this man had to be a citizen, a neighbor, a companion, and a friend; he had to continue to play that same role, to avoid all the trouble which would ensue in a discussion of his case by those whose capacity of spiritual intellect was in the Egyptian darkness of *felt*. Out of that Egypt was the Son called. Felt being *left*, those Egyptians got left, and were afterward swallowed in the C they read.

They read the swallow at the core, and understood the bull neck of Moses, and why many were made Jews on that day as described in the book of Esther.[1]

The Sun is an indescribable center of an electrical focus of currents from the planets. Those planets contribute to the sun's heat and receive its rays in return.[2]

Spots on the sun are an illustration of the law of the heating and cooling of planets by the change of poles.

Gravitation is accelerated by a vacuum in the center of the earth. It is adhesion of magnetism. Earthquakes, are the result of correcting time on the orbit.

Local. Lo see all. For the town of Reading, read in G; for Malden, see maul and den. For Melrose, M he L rose;[3] for Brockton, ☉ rock tom. For Waltham, double you all *th* Ham. Pittsfield is the pit of death — ℙ *it*. In this way apply all syllables to myths, and see the connecting circumstances by name and numbers.

Appalling, is a Paul in G. The apple is in G, the sun fruit which all souls eat of in the law of seven — the chromatic scale of numbers set to G. See Fig. 3.

It is seen in the word *fate*, that all F s must eat of that same ogee — the hollow and round of the serpent of time, in the place prepared for them after they leave the body. There will be no dodging it. The D oh G, is the death ogee — the serpentine mould = M oh you L death.[4] M you old.

---

[1] Est is east to west. Ast is the reverse, *under.*

[2] *Re* † urn.

[3] Roe see.

[4] Change to larvæ from sunshine.

The simple representation of the cruise, was ℙ; a P cut into an F. It has been marked in the sand every 2000th year since then, and is thus given to earth.

All representations of that cruise are correct for the times in which they were known, whether as a man spiked to a T, or burning on a pile of wood, or at a stake.

Four faced Janus is one, two, three, and four; add together and see 10 = ☉; see 10 mills (the 10 mil) is one cent — one sent — see N T. In addition to 10, God is to be counted *one*. This is carrying one for every 10.

Numbers tie by *fours* horizontally. When there are less than 4 figures, add cyphers to count 4 places. Put the one figure at the left of the perpendicular line, and a cypher to the left of *it;* then put 2 cyphers at the right of the line, and draw a line underneath. If 2 figures are used, place them at the right of the line. Face south with this T square work.

$$01|00 \qquad 21|00 \qquad 19|00 \qquad 21|01$$
$$\overline{1\,00} \qquad \overline{3\,00} \qquad \overline{10\,00} \qquad \overline{3\,01} = \text{ 4 JANUS.}$$
$$☉ \qquad\qquad\qquad\qquad ☉ \qquad ☉$$

See why 2001 is the first year of the first century again. See why $4 \times 4 = 16$, the ark.

See the numerals in the word Noah.

$$N \; O \,|\, A \; H$$
$$\overline{14 + 9} = 23, \; 2 + 3 = 5 \text{ the } ₤.$$

The O in Noah is a cypher.[1]

---

[1] By leaving the cypher in Noah, Nah is left; if this be reversed, the syllable Han appears; which put with itself, gives the word Hannah. First one way then the other — the suffer on the cross. The H as silent, leaves anna. In this manner, all Bible names have their origin. The cypher and silent H dropped from Noah, N A is left. N suffers the A as ⱥ twice, and gets two A A s thereby — a day circle of light as two D D s = ☉. Those two A A s are (is) M the 13, the sun; here is M and N; use the 2 sticks left across the A A s, and the pen for a third stick and spell M A N.

The reason for the disagreement in the computation of gene-alogies from David, is seemingly so. It is the different ways of computing that time by 3, 4, 7, 12, etc. It is done by letters in names, all meaning 49 years.

Adam was Eve also, — the twin. Eve was the darkness of his first life, the system he was married to. In *light*, find ghilt, guilt, gilt. All these names fitted the aspect of the heavens on time. Those stories are different ways of describing advents, and their consequences, and are not a history of the earth and its inhabitants in any other way.

Mankind kill each other because they do not see that *this* man had to have so many names. See snatch a rib, see king, see nack a rib = Sennacherib.

In Joseph is hose — the calf — leg. Then there is left the J — the fist of the Almighty and the P.

So it is all through the Bible. Those names of persons and localities are a time as well as a place. The same names apply to people and localities, as well as to things of spiritual essence.

See that *loaf* and *sas*, are in ass and foal. He rode into that city of spiritual knowledge by the eating of the menu ; lo a F he was ; time, A and S.

Jerusalem is that condition of spiritual knowledge, and a word that will be better understood out of the flesh.

J he are, you sa L he M.[1] It is God the Father and the Son as N with the pen. Names of localities in this country are astrologically adapted, the same as were those in the East.

The surprise of the wise people of that time to find the sun the star, and that the ro of the zodiac was the Bethel,[2] was the foundation for a short story.

The raising of Lazarus was a story of the same death. In that name is the razar L us. U S is the unity.

Those who, in their imagination, build scenes of 2000 years ago, may as well see the same things in the light of reason as to believe that all nature was suddenly convulsed, which all could see, but none would believe.

---

[1] The same as JEHOVAH-JIREH.
[2] ☉ he *th* hell.

The veil was rent and that soul went into sheol, hades, and hell.

The earth did quake the same as it always has at the return of the same period.[1]   An earthquake at the present epoch in which 20,000 people are estimated to have suffered, is not considered as any proof of an advent, nor was it at that time ; years elapsed, and the fulfilment of his prophecies was the proof of that advent.

People of to-day firmly believe that which the Romans could not, and those people were just as intelligent as the people of this age.

The surprise which awaits souls on the "other side" opher *th* hair, cannot be conceived here on earth.   It is the solemnity of a gigantic joke.   Who knows what a *joke* is in Hebrew?

If people of to-day could be shown an accurate picture of a scene in Aleppo, Syria, which took place 2000 years ago, would they be startled, or inclined to think of it as anything more than an every-day occurrence?

These musings should lead any one to see that the belief so strong in the mind is that which carries beyond this earth.

In Syria see Beraea and Aleppo.[2]   There is the Bear — he — A, and the O and apple.   The fitting of those names is not any closer than the work was.

The wrath of her who knows it all, was the foundation for Nazareth.   There is 14, and the razer — with fire.

The names which are in the several stories compiled as the gospel, are the result of the heavenly aspect of those days.   Time eye $\oplus$ O see.

"The stars shall fall."   People can not get up to them yet, so their language is brought down.   The forewarning was a seeming shower of starry sparks.

Man is looking for things on earth which he will see after D.   In this way he misses the mark.   The bull's-eye is the center of the tar G he T.

M is airy, *i.e.*, look through air to see the sun.   M airy, without the eye, is Mary, the darkness[3] of even in G $=$ evening $=$ Eve

---

[1] Italy 1886–7 $=$ 13 $=$ M.

[2] See map of ancient Roman empire.

[3] In *darkness* see the D ark and N $=$ 14, double timed.

N in G. Joseph was betrothed to that darkness in which was the child of light and knowledge. Joseph was David, he of the seven multiplied.

Mary is mar and the urn. To mar is to bruise; the same is the heel (heal) of time. Reverse mar, and see Ram. Mar with the serpent is Mars. The Ram buts; the reverse is stub. Stub is $ hub, and *hub* is the center of the wheel — the double you heel — heal of time.

Adam fell at Pisces, and went to the A — the sun, and could get no farther; was stopped by the sun; it was his dam — the A dam.

He, by coming to earth again, becomes his own father; and he was the womb man, woe man and woman; so he is always his own mother. By twins, he is always his own brother, and as the woman (Eve), he is always his own sister. See the 4 ways of relationship in the one head — the subject of mythology.

These things all fit further along, where language is taken in at one glance, and where it can be known without having to stop to study it.

Use the tops of the two PP s for DD s. Use the bottoms (stork) for X, see ◁ X ▷. D is X,[1] and T is R by putting the serpent on to T as $ = $ = ℞. *re* add (read) D he X and T he R, *i.e.*, D E X T E R.

In the foregoing (4 going) is to be seen an illustration of one letter becoming another. This law has but one weak place, and that place is only seemingly so to man. It is the law of the cruise, and no road but death (the O) will give it in detail — the death tale — the *re* tale — the mean and small way of parting with the jobbers' wares, the effects of Job, the middle man.

The word cruise, without the eye, is *curse*.

See the abomination unto you — the turkey. See all of his parts, and name them. See the strut is the $ rut. The rubber[2] is on his knows, and the prime in G brush is at the double you[3]

---

[1] By death it becomes the 2 sticks of T = X.

[2] The rubber is the last game.

[3] W means you double in purgatory, and become as the angels in heaven — twined.

ish — the lucky bone.[1] He is one type of the suffering Job. He has the F A N, the narrative, and the gobble — as Job gobbled down the menu of the tree. Job's patients were all mankind. A patient without the eye is a patent. The pay tent is in sheol.

In this way examine all things by naming the parts, and see what it is to offer these things as a sacrifice. Offer is off of the usual way of thinking of them by a low base of land gauge. Here is the so-called ignorance of past ages.

Jupiter is the name by which both Father and Son are known. That name gives the understanding of unity.

Pan is at the head of the 12 as 13 the sun.[2] 14 is connected with the word Son. In this way Pan is Jupiter.

All things are blended together in this same way, and is especially noticeable in gradations of pronunciation.

In Pisces and I H S see feet *ish* — fetish and his feat — feet. In this way read the law to suit the fancy — fan see — Pan see.

"The pool of Siloam." ℗ ool of Time, the eye and *loam* — the earth. The death at Cancer and the descent into hell was the pool.

℗ ool. That spear on the ℗ and the shepherd's crook put with it make another P. The two P P s make a B and the two edged sword — the two pen see — the spear with which the Dragon was slain.

In this temple must all syllables be put in place to have an understanding of the absolute law of God to man in the language he uses for his earthly convenience. The grind of this wordy mill is here and beyond.

This orthography is alluded to all through the Bible, and gives it that air of sacred mystery which man feels, but cannot tell why.

All words which have ology for an ending, are for all ogee = O G the serpent ; graphy is the O and spiritual knowledge beyond. V becomes F, and F ph.

The word God is the word for people of the earth to use, and

---

[1] Two ways from the spade.
[2] $13 + 14 = 27 = 9$, the eye.

is that which they are allowed. JEHOVAH is not for mortals to utter.

In the word *selfish* see elfish — hell fish, that which swallowed Jonah. In *swallowed* see S W allowed — aloud. S W is time you double, if you D O — do.

That L fish will swallow[1] every soul now living, as it has always done in the past.

E is sun in Leo. A is sun in Aries. U is the air.[2] E A U is the O in dialect, and is the hole and entrance to God.

Dialect — Die A he see †.

Man is always looking for chaos, as a proof of an existent God, — that very thing which does not take place because there *is* an existent God. God's works are used as a proof that there is no God, because man has never seen anything other than God's works to compare them with. He unconsciously desires proofs of no God, in order to prove to himself that there *is* a God. This is the result of his expecting chaos.

It is in his nature to be thinking of chaos in the future, because he is in the scale of progression, and is to see wonderful things of which he has only an instinctive imagination while in the flesh. Man's disbelief in a future is largely due to the misrepresentations of that condition by those who were in ignorance before him.

Can man do away with the law of lye, grease, and soap? If not, how can he escape the ash-water of his record, unless he mix with the grace of God and see *so* a ℘. For this comparison people did take umbrage 2000 years ago, and the vengeance of God has followed them ever since.

They said it was too small, and not worthy of the God whom they worshipped; yet they would admit that there was nothing too meek for Moses.

Souls have to get down lower than that comparison before they triumph in the silent H. See what it is to be born again — all in the she hall — sheol.

See that the advent of 2000 years ago was, where historians

---

[1] Swallow is in the core — sign Taurus.

[2] These 5 months are pebbles — P bulls for the sling.

can find some connections by war and disasters. He was of
Carthagenian[1] blood, born in Aleppo, Syria. Bethlehem was
the star route of his spiritual birth.

The ancient Romans acknowledged that God caused war, and
fought both sides. They opened the door of the temple of
Janus until peace, as an acknowledgment; but they would not
believe that he was the same to the black man as to the white.

People of this age should realize that the black race have been
the Jews for the past 2000 years, thus avoiding that error of
Rome and Greece.

The blacks sound D in place of *th*, and give B for V. Thus
is the soft blend of dialect divided among God's children.

They are called the children of Ham. See the pun is meant[2]
of that race. Pan is meant, fan is meant, *ban*.

The same warning is again here given, as at every such time
since the history of man. These things should be looked to
with reason and understanding.

---

[1] See car = are *th* age A G he.
[2] Punishment for unbelief.

CHAPTER XXIX.

By names, dates, and numbers, see the signs of this epoch of time. The combination cannot be unravelled by man in the flesh; but he can see a mix of names in daily news, and he has history to look over, in which is plainly written the book of 8 — of fate.

The unison of language (as shown in this work) is the way to find the unalterable law of God, and the way to see his dealing with man by that law.

This double reading is the "sign of Jonah"; always and forever the same — the double hautboy of Pan; 2 ways for earth, and 4 ways for the passage over the Styx by the in die A rout,[1] which is sure to be on time in the future, as it has never failed in the past.

The way the Romans read astrology was their fig-tree. Those "figs" (figures) was the way they built in the alphabetical law. They had lost the art, same as now. They did not see the simplicity of it.

The cursing of that fig-tree was the same as the cessation of work on the Tower of Babel — tower of babble — talk. They studied the double read, and admitted that they knew not what they said. Their language was confounded. C on founded — founded on C, the reed way they read — red.

The P roof (proof) of the double read will be the eat in G (eating) of music in notes of prince see P all and in T he rest — principal — principle and interest.

Fig. 18, is the two hawk-feathers used by the Egyptians to illustrate the eater piece of time in the adjustment; add the A to ment — meant.

Those two feathers mean the difference between the 8×8 square, and the 5×13 oblong square, as shown in Fig. 13.

---

[1] India.

Rameses was he who saw the Ram in the spiritual existence. No matter how many kings took that name afterward. He was the real Sennacherib also.

G all on, is a gallon. On gall.[1] From this, and with it, is the 4 quarts which it contains, *i.e.*, the 4 quarters of the square cross. They are Pison, Gihon, Hiddekel and Euphrates. Havilah is the circle around the whole as $\oplus$, and the circle of the neck. See havalock.

The goat — Pan. Me knee me knee † kel — kill you far sin. Mene Mene Tekel Upharsin — you pass in — to sheol — the O.

Thy soul shall froth, foam, and effervesce in purgatory and hell. Arising again to that land of fire, the seven churches of Asia, where all souls become spiritual Paraisians — Persians.

The "boils of Job," was this same overflowing in mead[2] — meadow — the swamp and marsh from which come flags and cat-tails.

The word dynasty, means the ash death, and should be a period of 2000 years. "There was war in heaven,"[3] is the time of making things *even* at the time of the die nasty ; the simplest way to unravel the Bible, is the sure and the truthful way. In *cursed*, is the cure, time, and death.

The man in the atlas of the heavens, is the sun man in his different characters and names as he goes through the 24 months' experience.

Tales in mythology are connected by stating some relationship with the names of the characters of some more ancient story, to show their mythical meaning.

Esau had a remarkable head of hair when young, and of air and H when old. This is why pictures of apostles vary as they got V airy. An *apostle*, means a part of the whole; in that word see post — P oh $, and Æ with the L for surety.

All have to bear those twelve different characters as they pass along, following their file — life — leader.

---

[1] The gall — gaul of the live ℞ .

[2] Medes.

[3] War in heaven is † sun and ℞ .

All souls will be Thomases after death. The reality is so far beyond the strongest belief on earth, that the bodily life will be counted as doubting. All are Peters, and Judases, and will sustain those characters in sheol. They are all Alpheuses. They see the sun in Alpha and Aleph the bull. See why Alpha becomes Aleph.

See introduce. Duced in the T roe. D you see law, is duce. Duce, is *two* — the double nature, because of suffering in that roe. In T rod, D you see £. In trod you see the £ cud. D you see ⊄ = see you ⊕, cub.

Menu, men you — mean you. This word is of the eating of the fruit of the tree in the G hard den. M he N you. An acknowledgment that M is N, and that the *you* here meant is he who did eat, will explain the word in part.

M becomes N, and is of and with the U, and U is the Holy Ghost in the law as revealed[1] to man. That menu is the fruit of time which no man can touch until he surely dies. He is then driven out of the G ℞ den, and sees that D is N. He finds every act of his life laid open, naked — $ ark — and gets his apron for shame — H same.

He eats of the tree (three[2]) in the airy space of sheol, and chews the Jew cud in caverns of earth, the place of hades.

Ancient pictures which show angels in the background have sheol for a basis. Wings are the same.

Those which have Astro connections can be easily understood to mean the calendar man.

Vulcan, the forger, is he who had to bear all the names of a 2 years' course — the 4 cube of the alphabet. From this is forgery when another name is used in fraud.

Forging is "smithing"; because he of many names understood the weld of the tire, the hammer and heat of Orion — iron — the steel — st eel — steal of the *th* eye he F (thief) who was forgiven on the cross in the sunlight of the heavens. In this way read myths with an understanding that the *seeming* whole, is but a part of it.

---

[1] Re vealed, calf, see half — D.
[2] Golgotha.

All the signs of the heavens are chained together electrically, and together they are the great "cats' cradle," a web, and *the* web. He who suffered all of those signs was stirred by that web, and thus found the 4 meanings of words and their connections; and it should be easy enough to see why the wordy man of his time was a Webster. The man next to him was Johnson, because of the son John soon to come.

Events have all been wove together as 4 warnings since the 10th century, gradually growing more perceptible.[1] Always by the mix of names and figures in civil affairs, as well as in war and pestilence.

The knowledge of these things is building the temple of the Lord, and must have a foundation. The foundation is the connection of events in the mix of names and numbers.

Place ain[2] on the alter, and see Cain. The mark placed *upon* him, was you P on him. He was born for G, and slew his first life. He was a wild man, *ish* M he all.[3] He slew A bel — B e LL.[4]

As none can approach the eye, E is used; it is the law, and in that way *ain* becomes ane, cain, lain, lane — the straight and narrow way.

Million, is eye on mill. Mill, is the great universe.

United, is the *re* verse of untied; the same of unite and untie. Verse, is *serve*. Observe, is serve Ob — the serpent. In *pen*, see that P is N = 14. Shoro, is time, hor and O = 15.

The "signs of the times," can be understood as the double read of Jonah, and they always indicate the overruling power of him who is never changeable — change a ble, change a bell — change a bull *never*.

Taurus is there the same as when placed there in and of the law, and he who was od in, and bald R[5] found the difference between the S not and the S $\maltese$not of the real cat R. He was

---

[1] P he are see he P T able — a bull.

[2] Ain, is the veil; in veil, is Levi — Pisces.

[3] Ishmael.

[4] Triumph over hell.

[5] Odin and Balder. God in Scandinavian folk lore. F all $\maltese$ lower; lo double W he R.

the same Elijah who suffered the blaze of hell and the dell, the blaze dale of I N R I.

Sun rise is also sun set to the inhabitants of the earth, as they severally see it; and just as simple as this is, just so simple are all of those things which men quarrel about, and murder each other by thousands. Thus what is a lie on earth, is truth in heaven, where the whole circle is seen at a glance.

He rested on the seventh — seven and *th* — fire; time, even, and fire. 1, 2, 3, 4, 5, 6, 7; do re mi fa sol la si. Si is time and the eye. He rested the H (8) on those seven, for they were the foundation of everything, and coupled the octave from A to H, and H became the bottom-stone of the foundation for another octave.[1] So seven days are a week, and the 1st day is the 8th again. The meaning of the first of Genesis is, that music is the law of the construction of the firmament. Genesis is generation by heat — H eat all of it — the heat ℞ piece — death and beyond.

Musicians know that in an octave there is something to be disposed of.[2] That *something* is the same cater piece — re eat a P see. The same is in mathematics as placed with the revolution of heavenly bodies. It is the surplus power always driving southward toward the dung gate of the temple from which it returns again to the head of the reign.

And the evening and the morning were the fourth day.[3] The *4th* daze way of fire; everything reads four ways. *Th* is fire from heaven, no matter in what word it may be found. The fifth day is in the law, and so on.

The serpent was more subtile than any ☉ he a ♂ (beast) of the field.

The serpent is the sub tile, the bottom rock, the foundation of the law of God, the sub base of the music; in *it* is the accurate crossing of orbits and everlasting life by correct time in divisions.

The sign of Libra is two sticks; one is bent in the middle, so

---

[1] In octave is O see V and eat; also death (oc), vat (bat), and the law — ℰ.

[2] Easily found in the tuning of the piano.

[3] One half of 8 the temple of a day.

when lain across the other, it will not touch; meaning a balance in the heavens and no clashing of orbits.

The mahl stick,[1] in connection with the arm, forms the cross; it has that name, because the old name for and of the suffering cross was Maahl. See Maul, Mawl — M hall. The sun and temple is the M hall, and the temple of Mahal Taj is to be read " *the temple of the suffering sun man.*"

What is false? fall see. The fall of the year north is spring of the year south. In like manner does a man claim a lie oftentimes, because of his putting his knowledge and ignorance together on one side of the scale. The moon is his stopper, and he wants to see everything accordingly. Falsetto, F all see toe — Pisces; an octave higher.

All words spell as leading to spirituality through O. Æ, U, and I; these are the five vowels. V becomes B at the 10th sign, and vowels turn to bowels — the balance — scales of justice. In this same way all words change to a heavenly understanding.

The soft blending of the vowels will all be simple and easily understood in the shoals of sheol and the shades of hades.

Baldrick, zodiac. Bald R eye C key. B all D arie see key, the Nat[2] you are all, the key of C smote with the reed is read in O G, the serpent.

From and with baldrick is derrick — death he R ah I see key. By the four guys G becomes Y. The G eyes — the four ways — of the cross.

The angles of the zodiacal derrick were the pit, the furnace, the den, the cloudy pillar, and mount Sinai. The angle of the law of ꓒ and Q rolled away the st one — stone; meaning death, and no man saw it.

The law was received at the place of derivation; deriver, the river of death, the Styx.

Deride. As long as man rides D, he can mock and scoff; but when ꓒ rides him, he will know the difference between impunity and Imp unity, and between deep read and D bread as ꓒ breed. It is the red C, and the shepherd's crooks with the

---

[1] Rest stick for the painter's arm. [2] Nathan — nay *th* a N.

st half — the staff — the pen; the dividing asunder — the two-edged sword.

The testament is composed of many tales which are, of themselves, quite short; they are put together to appear like one continuous history of a life.

The beheading of John the Baptist is the ash death of the same man, and the raising of Jairus' daughter is another.

See what a *daughter* is by Hebrew pronunciation: a D aught he are, a D ot T he R and so on.

In cavalry is Calvary — see all very, the ride of Pegasus in sheol; triumph in November — the bow man.

The blend of Hebrew can be seen by the most simple form possible of following up rhymes, as — its a nose you,

its an O shoe,

its snow shoe,

its no shew,

its know shew,

its know no its you,

its han oh *shoo*, and away goes the spirit from earth. This can be varied until the starting point is lost, but yet the connection kept good.

It is in the soul's experience as it leaps from the nose at the thirty silver [1] pieces into the vat of heavenly vocabulary, where there will be no more doubt about the upper room and cloven tongues of fire.

The soul will experience the Killing of (at) the Passover, the Martyrdom of the Twelve, the Eating of the *Last* Supper, the Sacrifice of Iphegenia, the Pyrrhic dance, the Flay of Alex,[2] and all such descriptions of that cruise as have been given from time to time in the history of the earth.

Because of a wordy resemblance of these things betwixt heaven and earth with earthly matters, those things have the stamp of bloodshed and suffering.

That similar things have happened on earth is true, because of the blend of language. It has always been the work of the

---

[1] As Judas — at the 1st of Arez by the sun circle.

[2] Skinning of the Assyrian.

devil, because man has been willing to give up to him. The D is the only letter accessible to man; the O and the D — the D and the O is his tonic and D read, *dread* — do for bread.

Dread must be *bread*, and from heaven; it is the man A — the sun man who always gives it all ways by the bevel ☉ instead of the devil[1] (◖L).

Leave hell, leave L is the level; and when applied to *level*, is eve = darkness — felt — left — L he F T.

In past ages unbelievers worked their way into power by the aid of the devil, and did most horribly butcher their fellow-men, and at the same time use the story of Cain for a text, when preaching to those who did believe and were saved. So it will always be, when men get excited, and think to make the most of life by making an exhibition of the power of the D.

The D is half a loaf; divide the word *loaf* in halves. Lo aF is seen — the weakest letter. In *loaf* is foal and fal O — fallow ground — the G round by the bridge of salvation — the ⊕ ridge; the ridge of that ⊕ is the pole route of they who are cyphered — see high fired out into the northern light of eternal heaven.

M he a N mean;[2] he who solves the riddle in this mean, close way of mean time, by silly bles, ples, fles — the tail and tale — the narrow T eye V.

Conjunction is see on June see † eye on — the but (tub), the and (Dan), the conjunction of heaven, earth, and hell.

Sodom and Gomorrah. So death O am and G oh M horror; the horror of M = 13. One turned and looked back and ⊕ came a pillar of salt and salvation. The wife of square ots Lots — the result of death in the Styx, J or dan — Jordan — J and or = gold.

F with lee, is feel. Lee is a place of wreckage, and F is the weak letter. Flee (flea) is the leap at the mend of time between the moon and sun; the hopper through which all souls go into the mill for purification. The jumping flea is the type; thus it is seen that all words are types of things further along in the soul's progression.

---

[1] Manna in the wilderness.

[2] Meaning mean in G — this — † I H S — *ish* way — the fish way, the whole the whale.

Put the word *text* upon the alter. The T T s, are the equinoctial points of Aries 20th, and Liber 20th — the 20th letter twice. X is the equatorial line across the ecliptic. E is the ⊙, the weasel of the whole, the same as the whale, where the hole is punched in the square to give a corresponding circle.

With ☐ (E) the word Lord is put, for it is the law of destruction to make things even.

By way of the precession of the equinoxes, the land gauge of the word *text* becomes varied, although the word itself remains the same, — the *theme.*

The precession, is the chewing of words and sentences into silly bles, ples, fles, and that work of precession, is the work of precision on the pole of the heavens where the work of blending is going on forever.

One letter becomes another, one syllable becomes another, a letter becomes a syllable, and a syllable becomes a letter, — all constantly changing in the eternal rounds of the precession of the equinoxes.

Precession of language, has its adjustment on the zodiacal belt, refracting on to the pole of the heavens. The pole line runs to the small dipper, which is ℙ — F and P together, where the law comes from.

Every sentence that man may say has three meanings other than the one he himself thinks he comprehends ; this is because of four-faced Janus at the head, and the law of four.

The twelve months' voyage in sheol, are twelve fords, straits, sounds, bridges, and all names of places which connect, making conjunctions, and are to be so allowed in Hebraic. Allowed, is hallowed — H allowed — all owe D, Hall O wed.

Put the word *ford* on the alter, and see the F from the left leaves ord ; there is od and the healer. Reverse ord, and see dor = larvæ ; the circle of twelve, adds O to *dor*, and gives door to the doer. Do ℞, and the spirit enters another sphere at *last* = L as †.

Every letter and syllable should be put on to the alter in God's temple and there H allowed. Allow every letter to be doubled, and put upon repetition; and every syllable punned, rhymed, and placed in the law of God to man.

$$ \text{⋇ P . ⟲ + ⋆ △ □} $$

An ancient sign for a butcher's shop; read from the right.

Weasel lamb and trip.

We sell Ham and Tripe.

Wheze, el am, and tri P.

Whezze hell am, and dry P.

The triangle is a lamb. To put that lamb on the altar, is to see the *word* altered — all T he are hed.

The triangle and lamb are the two words in one to alter.

The 3 sticks of that angle, is the tripod — the perfect $\bar{\top}$.

The body of a fleshy lamb, with all its namable parts, is to be read, as its bleat, is *table.* The grub (G rub) enters the nose (knows) and gnaws the brain.

The body is doby [1] — the D boy Isaac.

In this way go on finding the fit of all parts in the law of land gauge Hebraic — he bray I see. This is typical of the sacro $\bar{\top}$ ice of the lamb.

Facing south in the temple,[2] the crescent is seen over the right shoulder. The half moon is the D. Notice the direction of the bow side.

After the moon dam comes the sun dam; or in other words, after Diana comes Apollo. The sun is 13, the lucky, after the soul leaves the body. Luck, is the square uck; the hang on Haman's gallows — the you see ⋆.

The "bridge" is from 12 to 13 — Pisces to Arez; 13 ties up as Jupiter — $1 + 3 = 4$. He declares that by his one in 4, the 4 shall be one; so 13 becomes 1, the ace — sun.[3]

The mean and close way in and by which God regulates distances of orbits, is mean enough for the salvation of the hor;[4] it is meantime.

Hor, is what man can see only. The eye and D make *horrid.*[5]

---

[1] The daub of the paint with a *good* body.   [2] The open air — Mars Hall.

[3] One day spot — daze pot — D ace P oh †.   [4] Horologia, temple time.

[5] † makes torrid.

In this way of placing syllables for the future, is the connection to be found betwixt heaven, earth, and hell.

People are continually speaking Hebrew, and giving the law of God. What they say and do, is a forecast of the future on earth and beyond.

What they *do*, is dumb language. D you M, dumb. M you M, mum. The sunny mum way of muming F air — fare, for Jews to chose and chew — see hew of the acts — ax — the pi O near — pioneer — pi on ear.

See mixed and mixture. Ture is true. T U R E is pronounced as *chewer*. It is the chew of the Jew. In chew, see hew of the acts of H he double you — hew. T you are he, T you *re* at the cross.

The difference between the utterance of chewer (ture) and sure, is the break at the st. S is the 19th and T the 20th centuries; together they are ‡ the serpent and cross.

Sure, is the ruse of the shewer — the time hewer. He shews the shew bread — the ☉ read. Shew, is she double you. The U double on the T x in the she hall — sheol — the T x sure, T x chewer — T x T you ℞ □ — texture of the gar meant. The T weed[1] at the gar den.

Weeds, thorns, and thistles are all seedy, and the ear *th* brings them 4 *th* — earth brings them forth.

In Fig. 20, I N R I has the same meaning as the four rivers of Eden, with the addition of the diagonal — the X.

The two I I s are the pole and the sun in the east. All mankind are facing west and walking the ball as it turns toward them, as by the way they were cast in the matrix of the zodiac.

From this earthly adjustment the soul must be turned on the crosses in the progressive way from earth to heaven, and all start as F, the weakest.

With this turning on the cross, earthly language turns also, and thus the soul sees its past life all reproduced and adjusted with itself on the four-spoke wheel, the four-spoke way of the speaker who will speak as others have spoken before — ☉ 4 — ⊕.

---

[1] Tweed — dewet — duet — 2 ways of reading.

An elf is a soul just from the body ; an F from a P, done as ꟼ. Add the right angle (chopsticks) to F on the left and see L F. Add the law (⌐) and see E L F.   Add time and see S E L F.

NORTH

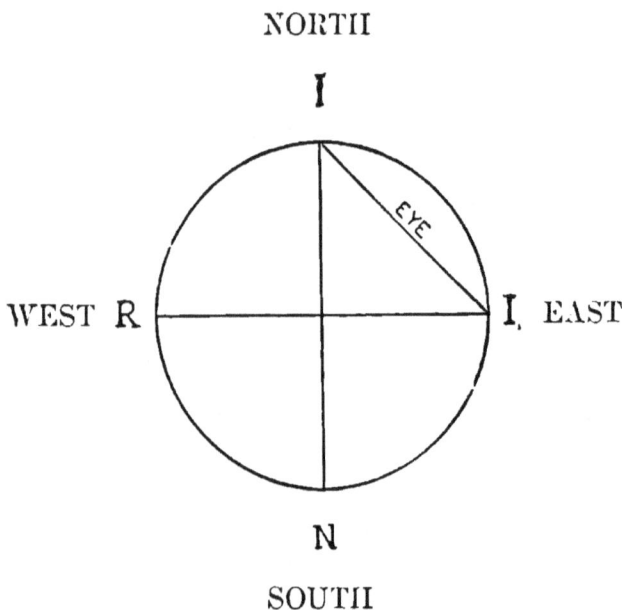

Fig. 20.

F air eye, fair I see, farie see, fairy see.   Amid sobs and convulsions, because of the reality of their fate, those fairies go into real hysterics.   His terror see — Thamaz.[1]

That terror is the T error, and is unerring.   One suffered on that T and tells it to man.

A part of mankind have longed for an explanation of these things, and have suffered in doubt ; while others have believed in seeming impossibilities, and were satisfied.

He square F — E L F.   Elf, elfish, hell fish, the same one which swallowed Jonah.

An elf is a soul just out of the clay.   It is astonished to find more than five senses, and all so A cute.   It is in the happy state of punning and matching the incidents of its past life by

---

[1] Bull terror — terrible.

rhymes, which is the elementary[1] of heavenly music. He is a Temanite — † man hight.

Because of his acute senses he is pictured with long ears, goggle eyes, and a cherry nose. He has to own up to all of his past inward thoughts, as well as sins of bodily acts. He is on the torture rack, and everything has to be told — he forgets nothing.

His sac bursts, and he is cast to earth — to larvæ. He drifts to a place where the murky atmosphere fits his aroma. See brimstone fire and the lake — the L ache of Hyades. He meets the Holy Terror.

His toes are picked. The "cloven foot" is the split between life and death at the moony Tekel[2] place — at the see love N foot of the heavenly matrix. Of these things mayst thou eat.[3] The chewing of the *cud* is see you D.

A cupid is the spirit released from the larvæ shell in hades, and he follows the path of love by the way of the B O and ℞ O.[4] The glorified spirit is never pictured. It is beyond description, because there are no close types on earth. The catfish[5] is the water type of an elf, and the sculpin is the type of the elf's skin.

The all seeing eye being the head, and the head being He, Ɛ becomes I and *is* I. Thus is, is es. Es is se, and see C. B is *two*. B *is* see you T he. B is see you it — biscuit composed of 2 halves as ⊕.

In the word dictionary it is seen that death and the cross is the time and place where all type will be understood.

In anglo saxon see angle O and the sax horn — the time ax and trumpet of Gabriel. *Gab* ℞ I he L. The *last* trump sounds S hounds. That *last* trump is always played at Pisces; the game is *footed*, soles are turned, and all lights out at *taps*. Tap becomes pat, ah I see ⊀.[6] M a sun double you tap pan. The tap at the brad ford of Jonah.[7]

---

[1] Hell he meant airy.

[2] See the power of the Tekel and fall — the pulley = ℘ you † Υ.

[3] The "*body*" is the twelve signs which compose the matrix in which the soul is recast and born again; all eat of it, and ℘ ℞ † ache (partake) of the double you Υ (eye) in Ɛ = ▢.

[4] Bow and arrow.　　　　[5] Hornpout.　　　　[6] Patrick, Aries 17th = 8.

[7] The brad — the point of the gourd.

O A E U I is the way the five vowels run from earth out. For man here they run a e i o u w y. The soul takes them — first the A (sun), then the E (weasel), then the eye (I), then cast down to O (hades), then the U lifts up again. The first O is at death.

The angel (angle) of the Lord rolls away the st one (stone), and that stone becomes a *th* one[1] by purifying fire from heaven.

The weasel is the square of a life with the wafer[2] hole of time taken out in hades. In L, the ogee spell, the G O spell, will be the gospel understood and experienced.

Would the law of a civilized country allow of man's entering a temple with a mahl stick, and driving out those who bought and sold stocks? What would be the result if it were tried in any city in this country to-day? The Roman laws were more strict than those of this day. How then did it take place, if the Bible is true, and *it is true.*

Man will rather believe that that man was the leader of a mob than to consider it as a condensed passage to describe the general result of that advent.[3]

The " tables were turned on them," for by his coming they became unbelievers, whereas they had previously been *believers.* They were imperfect astrological readers. They considered the T as meaning the balance of Liber only, and they had lost the proper understanding of the double E — the oblong fold which means the doubling of a letter in the same syllable. See book of Sibyl.

They read the signs of the times by names, games, dates, trades, deaths, births, disasters, etc., as letters and numbers applied. See why they considered games of so much importance. The name of him who won (one) was of the greatest importance. They had some idea of an approaching advent, and were looking for signs of the times.[4]

They put on many knowing looks, went up on platforms, and,

---

[1] *th* one becomes thome, plural thomes.

[2] Wafer is the seal of the sac.

[3] Advent — V, add ◯ — V, add 10 — Ten. V ent ad and carry one for Ten — ent — enter — entre — three.

[4] They were the builders who rejected the stone.

facing east, did pretend to read by stars those very things which they tried to read by the sorcery of observing the combination of every-day life.

They thought things were either pro or con. They reckoned but two ways, and those they could not see.

All events are subject to four quarters above, and the same beneath. The dark waters are dar quarters — D are quarters. Dar is the same as there, or there are, thar. It requires the combined language of all the earth to give the law of four.

See is the light of the upper day, and *sea* is the darkness of the lower day; these two D D s make a twin day of twenty-four hours. This is to be applied to souls as they pass through the O, and on to their double life as twins.

The law has to read in halves to man for this same reason ; it fits his case here, and while here, because he is but half and sees but one fourth. He is always probing the law, and thinks it unreasonable.

See the reason for unbelief in the minds of many men who have, or seem to have, good judgment about wordly matters, and average good tact.

If a man were a $\odot$ instead of a D, and were millions of miles away from earth on the pole line, he would then see what the D s are fitted to here, and why the law has to read in so divided a manner. He would see the twenty-four hour circle, and see why cone changes to come.

If the law were given as though man were now even, it would be so far from fitting his case here that he could not accept it, and it would outrage the source from which it came.

Some people who have been moved to tears while reading of the hardness and cruelty of the Romans of 2000 years ago, suddenly find themselves doing the same thing, and for precisely the same reason. They are the assets of the riches of Job. They, with their long ears for musical language, said, " We hear enough."

Daniel in the den of lions. Dandelions for greens and flying seeds. All souls become " sunflowers," and this is why flowers are *roses;* they rose from the dead body, F lower = flower — flour from the grind of the mill in sheol.

Is any one so simple as to think the yellow seedy flower which grows in the garden is meant? Yet people will do the very thing in Biblical comparisons. They do not realize the four ways, and that the mystery of the future is blended with the present for a connection.

Simon he surnamed Peter. *Surnamed* is time you are named; *i.e.*, so much of the suffering time was Peter. James and John he surnamed sons of thunder; *th* is fire from heaven, and they (two months) were *th* under; under *th* for sixty days, so much of the cruise.

The people wished for bread made from stone. $ one is the stone, and D bear is bread = ⊙ read. They knew not (new ⊀ not) that the reed was the pen with which he smote the read, or that in smote was see tom and some T.

In T O M see two and four sticks. $2 \times 4 = 8$, the temple. The entire combination of sticks, numbers, letters, figures, or any way of showing the same, will always give the same names and law of perfection.

The word *law* is to be read the square, the sun, the LL = storks; the L L s are the †. The flanks and lapwing are the same. W double you there all the same in the law — lau — aul — awl.

Mankind have looked coolly on the three T T T s of Golgotha, and tried to comprehend the love of God in allowing his son to be slain for themselves that they might escape the same thing; thereby making the love of God greater for sinners, than for his only ⊙ gotten son. Not being able to see it in that light, they then say, the son was willing to die for them, for the love he had for the race; and in that contemplation they rest. The mysteries are beyond man's comprehension.

The law of the circle of life being closed or broken between Pisces and Aries, is in all life on earth; and is done by the sun, with the one exception of the owl family. See feet head, fetid, fœted,[1] fœted is all the broken house of Levi. *Th* eat head, T heat head, *th* at head is the fire of life.[2] Snakes have no such

---

[1] Feet *ish*, fetish.

[2] Th instead of fe.

like experience; they coil (see oil) up often enough to preserve the circle of life, and are the symbol of life and of time.

The elf leaves the "feeted" body. The cupid leaves the elf shell, and has the full bow (the circle), and the air O (arrow), and the circle forever made good, because in a sphere of airy circles. The rattlesnake has the warning of the goat (December) at the tail (tale), and the fangs of Aquarius (January) at the head = Janus. This is literally true in the H, and not a studied comparison.

In a cycle of 2000 years, the rattle comes at the 20th century.[1] The "slight warning" is his S (hiss) 4 *th* fly in Egypt. Egg why ℗ T. "And he shall hiss for the fly in Egypt." The blowing of the horn at the tale end of the 19th, is that hiss, H is S. *Th* is S. *This*, present time, is the sphyncter, the Sphynx and Phœnix of time. Understand the Phœnix park — P ark — assassinations.

"And there were giants in those days." The bodies are much larger than the souls while they are within those bodies. The Bible is a very much condensed work as it is; with which, consider that all of those words are but abbreviations of larger words, that all read four ways, that those four ways are connected by a circle, — the tyre, — and then think, "who by searching can find out God."[2]

See ticks; tick-tacks of time, and tactics of military;[3] the drill of Upton — up Tom from hard D[4]— up Tom from H, death.

Gold, is old G. The gold of that land is good. There is bdellium and the on X stone,[5] — the X on Ɛ stone.

All of the time stories in the King James Bible, can be understood to mean seven with the eighth added for one on

---

[1] In Gabriel on the alter, see gab, bag, ℞ eye he L. Gab, is talk, and bag, is the moonshine from which the ⚔at was let out = ⊕ is G = 7 × 7 = 49.

[2] The *last* trump, was king of spades = time, ℘ and hades, the triumph over the grave. The blowing of the red sea horn = read C horn with the set piece = pen.

[3] This comparison is a fit in the law of the signs of the times in forewarnings; the way things run by names. Every identical thing in the history of the earth has been, and is the same, and will continue the same, and man is to see the power of God thereby.

[4] Hardee's tactics.   [5] O necks stone.

which to place the eye, making nine — the cat, and the destructive bits thrown out. All told by different divisions of time, and all meaning advents and their result.

Man is subject to this law, and will be until he is over the last crossing where there is no "something" to fire out of music. There is the sapphire stone.

The cruise of Jason is to be considered differently from the passage of a soul through purgatory to heaven, for the obvious reason of his returning to earth. It is the same experience with the accompanying labor of the bodily voyage (on earth) and the spirit of Castor who gives the law, being from the highest in knowledge among spirits, mixed in the twin.

The two tales are in the Bible, and can be separated, or taken as one being a part of the other. Man should use reason about religious matters, as he does about worldly affairs, and not let his imagination lead him to expect heaven on earth, although it reaches to earth by the Holy Ghost which none but one man's eyes have seen in the flesh, and not another.

Man goes wild in what he names a belief; his belief never changes the law by which he is saved. In *saved*, is the vase (Y) and D — the only rout = tour = T hour = our T oh you R ah — A to H.

Some people suffer in mind with a fear of hell, because that they have not felt that "*change* of heart,"[1] which some claim to have experienced. That which is claimed as a change of heart does not alone save that soul from the most distressing and perilous voyage. A clean confession to the Holy Spirit of every little sin here on earth, with prayer, is a course for sinners to take. It is neglected because man is bodily blind to the spiritual ether in the air; one glance would fix him forever, but it is not in the law, or so to be. It is the soul's experience when it leaves the house of clay.

Dishonest[2] dealings between man and man are obstacles in the path to salvation. There is no act so small but that it is seen, known, and on record. When a man "beats" another, in such a way as to escape the penalty of the laws of man, his

---

[1] In heart is *earth*.   [2] D is H one st.

fellow-men say "he is sharp"; and give him credit for it, as though it were a fine accomplishment.

This is breaking the law of high heaven, and is a greater burden to carry through than that of him who, having broken man's law, has suffered the penalty on earth and goes out clean. Man is in a constant state of temptation to do sinful things, and none are free from yielding. Some yield to greater, and some to lesser. In *yield*, is Y and lied — die L — dial = 12.

The innermost thoughts of man against man, must be all reckoned as sin at the *last* day, whether they were accompanied by acts of the body or not. Such is the purity of spirits.

Here man will exclaim, "*None can be saved!*" Bear in mind forgiveness and a change of dealing. Upon *this*,[1] the Church is founded, and people become Christians. The "golden rule" comes from high heaven, and it is a sin to break it.

Born in a manger; in a man, G he are. In a stable, st able — time † a bull — ⚡ able — bale — Abe L. Abe ray Ham. Abel.

Paul was *this* man. Put *this* on the alter and see *fire is* — the digest and law. See Paul's acute talk to those doubters; it was full of the strength of the double reed, for he was the master of language.

He was the Matthew, Mark, Luke, and John; the four sea sons, the fore see son, the four C son of the divided year = ⊕. He could read the four ways of the trans pyre in G, the transpiring of transfiring. The spirit in the neck connected with the Holy Ghost was the source of his knowledge, the same as ever in the G man who is periodically born for it.

Theology — *th* all ogee — the serpent.

Prose ℘ rose from death.

Etymology — eat M all ogee.

In *rose*, is sore — the time ore — metal — met all.

Ogee — O G, is the foundation of hog. See why hogs will fight snakes, and absorb the poison of the rattlesnake without harm. The affinity of ogee the serpent with the letters O G does it. Thus grease blends with grace; grace on time will triumph over the sting of death — the line of Pison and Gihon.

---

[1] He who was forgiven on the cross in sheol.

The name of everything is its affinity, and connects with a future life. That life is not reached without suffering the law of destruction.

Swill, is the time willed out of the orbit by distance; blends in grease and grace.

Pocket, is the same as the pit.

Wagon, is the joker on G. That wag is on, then gone, and thus he drives the fiery chariot.

G, becomes itself single, in gig, the D ock † he ℞ s to double you healed (two wheeled) vehicle = V high see L he.

See the flounder with his **two** sides; he sees all one way. Thus all " little fishes praise God," and all things in sea and on earth the same by name and construction.

Monkey, is 13 (M) on key; the soul gets at the key in the sharp rays of sunlight in sheol on the surface of the air, the top of that in which he is now at the bottom, smothered in the flesh.

Man will weep at the recital of a tale in which is mentioned the stone which the builders reject, and is firm in his belief that it was all so; and yet, when he is confronted with the reality which the cycle of time always brings about, he would rather believe that it was *once* so, but never to be again.

He would rather continue to worship the same old images formed in his mind according to his interpretation of iron and brass than to take the trouble to find the foundation for his belief as given by the Prophet in the law from time to time, as cycle after cycle of time rolls on.

Man loves to believe in the has been and is to be, but he shrinks from the idea of the repeat of history, or the thought of discovering the epoch of the circle of time in which he lives.

Man worships his ideal as a law of nature; he cannot help it. The phenomena of his mind seems to be inseparable with his body, and he easily forgets that the Sun Man was very different in that respect. *He*, suffered the separation, and solved the riddle.

Man will admit that he was not like others, and will quarrel among themselves about what they think that difference was; as though it were necessary to know that which they cannot know, until such time as the soul is separated from the body; there the soul will be put on the cross, and find out the fact of one having suffered there before, and returned to the body on earth — the leader of the human race and the head of the church, whether recognized on earth or not.

It is in man's nature to expect all of the disasters of 2000 years to be thrown into one day, and that day to be the one in which the Archangel comes to earth. Some are suffering in the delusion of their imagination as they think of a God in perfection who is suddenly to precipitate chaos, and thinking of themselves as plucked from that vortex, while their fellow-man is burnt with the earth and blown away with the smoky chaff.

It should be easy for people to see that cold death will overtake them while in the same frame of mind, as it has always done in the past. See in F A N how the seed = see death is plucked, and the bodily chaff cast into outer darkness by the win oh in G (winnowing) mill of God. ₽ you are G ▢ is purge. Floor, F lower — hades.

As long as this earth is fitted for man, so long will the spirit Mercury return in *this* same way to regive the law in unspoken language; always teaching humility, and the way of the meek and lowly as the pathway to immortality and eternal life.

The extent of man's power to comprehend the incarnation is his idea of a holy spiritual influence which he himself sometimes feels. That sensation on his part, is the pressure of ◖, instead of ▢. See the difference is as ◖ compared with God, and *no* experience as a spirit out of the body or in it. A mere malty soul waiting for a release, and a re lease in the spiritual kingdom of God. The law of God in language, is the law forever, the same as found in Hebrew; in which, there is no

END.

DATE DUE

GAYLORD			PRINTED IN U.S.A.

www.ingramcontent.com/pod-product-compliance
Lightning Source LLC
Chambersburg PA
CBHW020548270326
41927CB00006B/770